Geographical Study Skills

PEARSON

We work with leading authors to develop the strongest educational materials bringing cutting-edge thinking and best learning practice to a global market.

Under a range of well-known imprints, including Financial Times/ Prentice Hall, Addison Wesley and Longman, we craft high quality print and electronic publications which help readers to understand and apply their content, whether studying or at work.

Pearson Custom Publishing enables our customers to access a wide and expanding range of market-leading content from world-renowned authors and develop their own tailor-made book. You choose the content that meets your needs and Pearson Custom Publishing produces a high-quality printed book.

To find out more about custom publishing, visit www.pearsoncustom.co.uk

PEARSON CUSTOM PUBLISHING

Geographical Study Skills

Core textbook for Geo1096

Compiled by
Dr. Simon Tate
University of Newcastle

ALWAYS LEARNING　　　　　　　　　　　　　　　　　PEARSON

Harlow, England • London • New York • Boston • San Francisco • Toronto • Sydney • Auckland • Singapore • Hong Kong
Tokyo • Seoul • Taipei • New Delhi • Cape Town • Sao Paulo • Mexico City • Madrid • Amsterdam • Munich • Paris • Milan

Pearson Education Limited
Edinburgh Gate
Harlow
Essex CM20 2JE

And associated companies throughout the world

Visit us on the World Wide Web at:
www.pearsoned.co.uk

First published 2011
This Custom Book Edition © Pearson Education Limited 2012

ISBN 978 1 780 16746 6

Printed and bound in Great Britain

Contents

Note-taking in lectures

How to refine what you hear into note form

The aim of lectures, regardless of discipline, is to present a topic for study in ways that introduce key points and develop understanding through explanation, provision of examples or citation of references for further reading. This chapter outlines approaches to attending lectures, and taking notes from what you hear and see during the lecture.

Key topics:
→ Your role in lectures
→ Approaches to note-taking

Essential vocabulary
Annotate   Concept map   Learning personality   Mind map   Verbatim

Lectures should be seen as a guide to a topic rather than the definitive or final word on a subject (**Ch 14**). The university lecture provides essential information delivered in a particular sequence for a particular course. In many subjects, the lecture is an introduction to the topic rather than a comprehensive analysis. For some subjects, lectures are often compulsory. This may be dictated by professional associations that validate many professional qualifications and is not simply a university regulation. Some students visiting the UK may have their attendance monitored as part of UKBA regulations (p. 23).

→ Your role in lectures

Lectures are not intended to provide you with a full understanding of the subject, and certainly not the total requirement for exam revision. Thus, some input on your part is assumed. Since you will attend many lectures in a week, maybe several in a day, it makes sense to keep some record of what you have seen and heard. It is important to consider what your purpose is when you take notes, since this will affect your strategy. For example, you may wish to write up the notes in a style that is more comprehensive and comprehensible to you. Alternatively, you may use the original lecture notes as the basis for note-making from texts cited from the reading list. In many subjects, this practice is assumed as part of the learning process.

Routine lecture note housekeeping smart tip

In each lecture:

- note the date;
- note the lecturer's name;
- note the lecture topic or title;
- number pages 1, 2, 3 . . . ;
- note down the aims of the lecture as outlined at the beginning of the lecture.
- keep a full record of what was said for future reference and exam revision;
- note key points to allow you to do follow-up reading on the topics in your own time;
- as appropriate record a constructed argument, a sequence of ideas or a process;
- as appropriate record information that will help you derive a proof or formulae.

Think about who you accompany in lectures

If you sit alongside students who are native speakers of English, then you will be in a better position to ask them for help with particular words or with comparing notes that you each took. If you sit with others from your own language community, then you might be able to discuss the points more fluently using your own language, but that means that you are not practising talking about your subject in English. Both strategies have merits and you need to decide which is better for you.

→ Approaches to note-taking

How you write down notes in lectures will depend on:

- your ability to listen for specific information and the thread of an argument, discussion or sequence of a process (**Ch 15**);
- the neatness of your handwriting;
- your particular learning personality or style (**Ch 13**);
- the styles of delivery you encounter in lectures (**Ch 15**);
- the subject you are studying and its conventions;
- the specific lecture content.

Notes made as a result of reading provide you with the chance to design a layout that reflects your learning style and understanding (**Ch 25**). This is less possible in a lecture because you are following someone else's logic without having the chance to reflect on this too much. As a result, the design of your lecture notes has to be spontaneous and is less under your control. However, as you become a more experienced note-taker, you will become more attuned to ways in which the format of the lecture can be adapted to particular types of note-taking design.

Table 16.1 outlines four different lecture delivery modes that are commonly used and makes suggestions as to how you might extract key information for your notes.

Table 16.1 **Note-taking scenarios.** Each lecture is unique and the strategies adopted by the lecturers will vary from individual to individual, topic to topic and according to discipline conventions. You will need to adapt your note-taking style to the mode of presentation, the style of the individual lecturer and the content. Four possible scenarios that you might encounter are shown in this table.

Scenario 1	Scenario 2	Scenario 3	Scenario 4
'Straight' lecture: delivered without handouts or special visual aids	Lecture supported with printed handouts	Lecture delivered using notes on a board or overhead transparencies	Lecture delivered using *PowerPoint* software
Listen for: • Aims of lecture or outline of structure of lecture. • Names of authors, dates of publication. This is the usual way of citing sources in a lecture. You will need to consult the reading list for details of title, chapter or page references. • Key personalities, dates or events relating to specific aspects of the topic. • Discourse markers – the signpost words (Ch 15, Ch 29) that indicate stages and shifts of emphasis within the lecture. • Structuring of an argument and the supporting evidence; stages of a process; sequence of events. • Repetition of points or oral emphasis using exaggerated stress or intonation. • Summarising of points at mid- and end-points in the lecture.	If handouts are available before or at the lecture: • Use highlighters to mark key points. • Use a contrasting colour, e.g. red or green, to annotate notes with additional information, examples or explanations given in the lecture. This will make it easier to distinguish from the printed text. • Make additions as described in scenario 1. If handouts are available after the lecture, use your own notes taken in the lecture to expand the lecture notes. **Warning:** Notes from lectures, whether borrowed from a colleague or made available by the lecturer, are not a substitute for attending the lecture. Lecturers expand on certain points or add examples to clarify understanding. They may also deviate from the notes and expand points outside the notes.	Follow scenario 1 but in addition: • Copy points shown on overheads as the skeleton for your own expanded notes. • For this kind of presentation it is sometimes helpful to work with a friend where one person copies the slide and the other notes what is said when the lecturer 'talks to the slide'. After the lecture merge the notes to create a more comprehensive record of what was actually covered in the lecture. To do this, you will need to work together in order to agree the synthesis of your notes and this will offer opportunities to discuss and clarify points. This process will reinforce your learning.	Use of this software provides a slick and professional presentation that permits good images of the detail of graphs or diagrams, and the lecturer can build these up stage by stage. However, this approach can often create an amount of detail that is very difficult to note down completely in the lecture. If this is the case for you, try to follow the steps for scenario 1 and ask for the *PowerPoint* slides to be made available for downloading before or after the lecture. This has cost implications but note that there are options to print out slides as handouts of two, three, four, six or nine slides to a page using greyscale or black and white rather than colour (Ch 26).

Figure 16.1 illustrates four possible formats for notes and suggests ways in which these different strategies can be used to suit different note-taking needs within lectures. Adding to these strategies, note-making approaches are covered in **Ch 27**.

Keyword notes

Topic   Lecturer   Date

Aims

- Good for lecture where there are clear divisions to its structure.
- Easy read-back using keywords in shaded boxes on left of the sheet.
- The printed margins could be used to separate keywords from corresponding text.

Concept maps/mind maps

Lecturer   Date

Topic

- Works best using page in landscape position.
- Good for the meandering lecture where there is back-tracking, re-emphasis and repetition.
- Suits some learning styles better than others.
- Easily annotated but can become cramped.
- Needs tidy writing.

Linear notes

Topic   Lecturer   Date

1. Heading
   1.1 Sub-point
   1.2 Sub-point

2. Heading
   2.1 Sub-point
   2.2 Sub-point

3. Heading
   3.1 Sub-point
   3.2 Sub-point
   3.3 Sub-point

- Good for scientific subjects and other subjects that follow processes or procedures where a hierarchy of events or stages is often relevant.
- Again, easy read-back using decimal notation to identify sub-points. A mix of numerical and lettered referencing (e.g. 1, 1a, 1b . . .) could also be used.
- Effective use of white space makes this memorable.

Matrix notes

Topic   Lecturer   Date

Aspect	View 1	View 2	View 3	View 4
A				
B				
C				
D				
E				

- Good for laying out different/contrasting viewpoints across a number of aspects of an argument. Works well if this is a declared aim of the lecture.

Figure 16.1 Note-taking strategies. Four models of note-taking showing the benefits of each style.

Tips for good note-taking

- Listen for and note the key ideas – avoid trying to write down every word (verbatim notes). It's impossible – you'll miss out on understanding ideas, explanations and examples.
- Develop a note-taking style that will provide you with notes that will be meaningful in six days, weeks or months.
- Cultivate your own 'code', for example:
  - underlining or highlighting points emphasised by the lecturer;
  - asterisks (*) for points or new words to look up later;
  - BLOCK CAPITALS for sub-headings or keywords;
  - special abbreviations for your subject that are in general use or that you create for yourself;
  - a symbol (e.g. #) that indicates your thought or response to a point made by the lecturer.

 Practical tips for attending lectures and taking notes

Prepare for the lecture. Try to read some fundamental background information on the topic. This could be the introduction to that topic in a basic recommended textbook or from a good encyclopaedia. Beware of internet sources, because these can be unreliable in terms of accuracy and truth.

Obtain supporting material. Some lecturers make use of virtual learning environments available in many universities to provide lecture notes, handouts, overhead transparency or *PowerPoint* slides before or after the lecture. Downloading this kind of material when it is made available may assist you to make more comprehensive notes. Note that the provision of this material remains at the discretion of the lecturer. If you have a hearing impairment, are dyslexic or have another visible or invisible disability, you may be able to request that lecture notes or handouts are made available to you before lectures. You should consult the disability support service in your institution with regard to any special needs you may have.

Select your position in the lecture. Choose a seat that allows you to see the whiteboard, projection screen or television monitor easily. Avoid sitting near the door, the back of the room (most commonly inhabited by the chatterers and latecomers) or underneath noisy air-conditioning vents. If you have a disability, you can ask for special arrangements to be made to enable you to access a lecture theatre or room without difficulty and also, if necessary, to ensure that a particular seat is reserved for you.

Use an appropriate paper size. A4 is the standard paper size for handouts and printers and so it makes sense to be consistent by using A4 paper and file size for your own notes. It is probably more economical to use narrow-lined paper with a margin, as this allows you to optimise the use of paper. Some subjects might require blank rather than lined paper to allow for diagrams and mathematical calculations. Otherwise, your own handwriting style and ability to write neatly at speed will dictate your choice.

If you are neat by nature, lined or unlined paper is probably not required (you can get more text on unlined paper!); if you are generally untidy in your writing, the lines will discipline your note-taking. Small reporter-style notebooks are not recommended, because the volume of notes that you will generate will fill one of those pads in a very short time.

Store your notes carefully. Decide on a strategy for filing your notes that is systematic and foolproof. Foolscap or A4 files with two holes are the most readily available and therefore cheaper. You may prefer to keep separate thinner files for each subject, or to use a single lever arch-file for a subject and use colour-coded section dividers to separate topics within the subject area. Get into the habit of filing notes immediately after the lecture so that they are not lost.

Adapt your style. There is no single way to take notes that will suit all styles, content or circumstances. You will need to adapt your style to suit individual delivery styles as well as content.

Write up lecture notes after the lecture. Views differ on this. You need to ask yourself a difficult question – what do you gain from this exercise? Some people feel that this is an essential aspect of the learning process, is an aid to understanding and aids their recall. Others start off by re-writing notes but quickly find that there is simply not enough time to revisit lecture notes in order to remodel them to make them neater, more legible or more meaningful. If writing up lecture notes is just to make your notes look neat, colourful or simply pretty, you need to consider whether the time might not be better spent doing some follow-up reading using your 'raw' lecture notes as a guide and possible skeleton for notes you make from sources (see **Ch 25**).

 Useful language for . . . discussing your notes

Context: these points might be discussed with a fellow class member.

My notes from that lecture are a complete mess [slang phrase]. Can I get together with you some time to discuss what you took out of the lecture?

I've found a good book in the library that covers this topic really well.

I'm going to experiment with a new type of note-taking this lecture. I'm going to try mind mapping. In case it doesn't work, would you mind if I copied your notes after the lecture?

(GO) And now . . .

16.1 Check availability of handout notes, overhead transparency or *PowerPoint* slides. Some lecturers will make these available before the lecture as handouts or as online files. If this is not the practice, you might consider asking as a group for this to be considered as an aid to learning.

16.2 Develop your note-taking skills. As with all skills, that of note-taking will not be acquired immediately. You will need to work at it and, if you are able to do so, you can do this by practising taking notes from one of the principal news broadcasts on radio or television. If you do this over a week or so, this will give you the chance to experiment with different layouts. If you listen to a broadcast at 6.00 p.m., for example, you can check your notes against a similar broadcast at a later hour in the same evening.

16.3 Collaborate on note-taking. Arrange with another student on your course to pair up for note-taking together in a lecture. For the first half of the lecture one of you takes the written notes, the other simply listens. At a mid-point in the lecture, change roles. At the end of the lecture, together work on the two half-sets of notes; develop these by adding your individual recollections for both listen-only periods. Photocopy the revised notes so that each of you has a copy. The value of this approach in that you will both have a richer, more detailed record of the lecture and you will have had to think further about the content and discuss the salient points. Overall, this will enhance your understanding and your learning.

Effective academic reading

How to read efficiently and with understanding

Whatever your discipline, you will find that you are required to do a lot of reading when researching. This chapter explains how to develop the speed-reading skills that will help you to deal more effectively with academic text.

Key topics

- Surveying the overall organisation of a source
- How to examine the structure of the writing itself
- Speed-reading techniques

Key terms
Blurb   Finger tracing   Gist   Terminator paragraph   Topic paragraph
Topic sentence

Much of the material you will read as part of your research will be journals, books, chapters, research papers and reviews written following traditional academic style, and may appear, at first glance, to be heavy going. However, by analysing the way printed academic resources are organised and understanding how text within them is structured, you should find it easier to read the pages of print in a way that will help you gain an understanding of the content, while saving you time.

● Surveying the overall organisation of a source

Source material may be suggested by your supervisor; alternatively, you may come across a resource in the library that looks as if it might be relevant. In either case, carry out a preliminary survey of the text to familiarise yourself with what the material contains. You can use elements of the structure to answer key questions about the content, as follows:

From Chapter 8 of *How to Write Dissertations & Project Reports*, 2/e. Kathleen McMillan & Jonathan Weyers. © Pearson Education Limited 2008, 2010, 2011. All rights reserved.

- **Title and author(s).** Does this text look as though it is going to be useful to your current task? Are the authors well-known authorities in the subject area?
- **Publisher's 'blurb' (book) or the abstract (journal articles).** Does this indicate that the coverage suits your needs?
- **Publication details.** What is the date of publication? Will this source provide you with up-to-date coverage? For books, is this the most recently published version?
- **Contents listing.** Does this indicate that the book or journal cover the key topic areas you need? Do the chapter or article titles suggest the coverage is detailed enough?
- **Index.** This applies only to books. Is this comprehensive and will it help you find what you want, quickly? From a quick look, can you see references to material you want?
- **References.** Does the reference list include a comprehensive listing of recently published work?
- **General impression.** Does the material look easy to read? Is the text easy to navigate via sub-headings? Is any visual material clear and explained well?

The answers to these questions will help you to decide whether to investigate further: whether you need to look at the whole source, or just selected parts; or whether the book or journal article is of limited value at the present time.

 What is your reading goal?

Always decide this before you start reading.

- If you are looking for a specific point of information, then this can often be done quickly, using the index, sub-headings or chapter titles as a guide.
- If you need to take notes from the source material, then you might read more strategically (see Table 8.1 and pp. 80-2).
- If your aim is to appreciate the author's style or the aesthetics of a piece of writing, then you may read more slowly and re-read key parts. Similarly, if your purpose is to identify key numerical data or follow the rationale of a discussion, then your reading may be slower.

Sometimes, different methods may be required, for example, in English literature, 'close reading' techniques. These specialised methods will probably have been as part of your introductory studies.

Reading and note-making

This chapter is concerned mainly with reading and comprehension as a prelude to note-making (**Ch 10**). While it is possible to read and make notes at the same time, this is not always the most effective form of studying, as your notes may end up simply as a rewrite of the source text. Notes framed after you have scanned the prescribed section of text will be better if you have a clearer idea of their context and content.

● How to examine the structure of the writing itself

Well-structured academic text usually follows a standard pattern with an introduction, main body and conclusion in each element (**Ch 20**). Sometimes the introduction may comprise several paragraphs; sometimes it may be only one paragraph. Similarly, the conclusion may be several paragraphs or only one.

Within the structure of the text, each paragraph will be introduced by a topic sentence stating the content of the paragraph. Each paragraph performs a function. For example, some may describe, others may provide examples, while others may examine points in favour of a particular viewpoint and others points against that viewpoint.

The function of these paragraphs, and the sentences within them, is usually signalled by use of 'signpost words', which guide the reader through the logical structure of the text. For example, the word 'however' indicates that some contrast is about to be made with a point immediately before; 'therefore' or 'thus' signal that a result or effect is about to be explained.

You can use this knowledge of the structure of writing to establish the substance of a piece of text by:

● Reading the topic and terminator paragraphs, or even just their topic sentences, to gain a quick overview of that element.
● Scanning through the text for key words related to your interest. This scanning may indicate particular paragraphs worthy of detailed reading. Sometimes headings and sub-headings may be used, which will facilitate a search of this kind.
● Looking for signpost words to indicate how the text and its underlying 'argument' is organised.

Reader as author

An understanding of the organisation of printed material and the structure of academic text are important for you as a reader or decoder of text, and they also come into play when you become an academic author and have to put your own ideas clearly – they help your reader (often 'the marker') to decode your written text.

Figure 8.1 shows a layout for a piece of text with five paragraphs, comprising an introduction and conclusion with three intervening paragraphs of varying length. Table 8.1 gives an example of an authentic text that demonstrates the structural organisation shown in Figure 8.1.

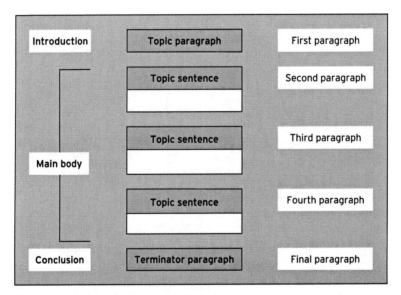

Figure 8.1 Sample textual layout. You can visualise the structure of any piece of reading material in a similar fashion.

● Speed-reading techniques

Before describing techniques for improving reading speed, it is useful to understand how fast readers 'operate'. Instead of reading each word as a separate unit, these readers use what is called peripheral vision (what you see, while staring ahead, at the furthest extreme to the right and the left). This means that they absorb clusters of words

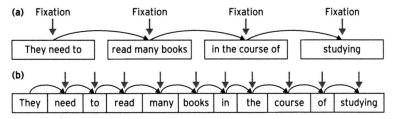

Figure 8.2 Eye movements when reading. (a) Reader who makes eye fixations on clusters of words. (b) Reader who reads every word one by one.

in one 'flash' or 'fixation' on the text, as shown in Figure 8.2(a). In this example, four fixations are required to read that single line of text.

A reader who does this is reading more efficiently than the reader who reads word by word (Figure 8.2(b)). This reader makes 12 fixations along the line, which means that their reading efficiency is low. Research has also indicated that people who read slowly in this way are less likely to absorb information quickly enough for the brain to comprehend. Therefore, reading slowly can actually hinder comprehension rather than assist it.

As a practised reader, you will probably have developed these fast-reading skills to some degree. They can be improved using techniques like the 'eye gymnastics' exercise in Figure 8.3. Other things you can do include 'finger tracing', where you run your finger below the line of text being read to follow your eyes' path across a page, starting and stopping a word or two from either side. This is said to increase your eye speed, keep your mind focussed on the words being read and prevent you from skipping back to previous sentences or jumping forward to text that follows. Some people find it helpful to use a bookmark placed horizontally along the line they are reading, because it makes a useful guide that prevents the eye jumping ahead of the text they are reading.

Origin of speed-reading

The basic techniques were developed in the 1950s by Evelyn Wood, an American educator. She set up institutes to teach students to develop an ability to read hundreds of words per minute. Those who have studied her method include businessmen and politicians, who have to learn to read lengthy papers quickly but with understanding. US Presidents Jimmy Carter and John F. Kennedy were both regarded as famous speed-reading practitioners.

Learning to read quickly	is a skill	that needs to be developed.
If you have to read	a new piece of text,	you will find it useful
first of all	to read	the first paragraph
and the last paragraph	of the section, chapter or article.	From this
you should be able	to gauge	the context
and general outline	of the topic under discussion.	While it is true
that all academic texts	should have been well edited	before publication,
it does not follow	that every text	will follow these conventions.
However,	a well-written piece	of academic writing
should follow this pattern	and, as a reader,	you should exploit
this convention	in order to help you	to understand
the overall content	before you embark	on intensive reading
of the text.		
When you are about to	take notes from texts	you should not begin
by sitting	with notepad ready	and the pen poised.
Certainly	make a note of	publication details needed
for your bibliography,	but resist the temptation	to start taking notes
at the same time as	beginning	your first reading of the text.
It is better	to read first,	reflect, recall
and then write notes	based on	what you remember.
This gives you	a framework	around which
you ought to be able	to organise your notes	after you have read
the text intensively.	People who start	by writing notes
as soon as	they open the book	will end up
copying	more and more from the text	as their tiredness increases.
In this case	very little	reflection or learning
is achieved.		

Figure 8.3 'Eye gymnastics' exercise. Try to read the text above quite quickly. Read from left to right in the normal way. The aim of the activity is to train your eyes to make more use of your peripheral vision when you are reading. In this way, you will learn to make fewer fixations on the text by forcing your eyes to focus on the centre of a group of words, which are printed in naturally occurring clusters - usually on the basis of grammatical or logical framing. It may be that you experience some discomfort behind your eyes, which indicates that they are adjusting to this less familiar pattern. If this is the case, you should keep practising using this text as a means of developing the speed of your eye movements.

Things that can reduce your reading speed

As well as trying methods to read faster, you should be aware of circumstances that might slow you down. These include:

- distractions such as background noise of television, music or chatter;
- sub-vocalisation (sounding out each word as it is read aloud);
- reading word by word;
- over-tiredness;
- poor eyesight – if you think your eyes are not 20:20, then it might be worth going for an eye test; your eyes are too important to neglect and a pair of reading glasses may make a huge difference to your studying comfort;
- poor lighting – if you can, read using a lamp that can shine directly on to the text; reading in poor light causes eye strain and this, in turn, limits concentration and the length of reading episodes. Daylight bulbs can also help to reduce eyestrain.

Increasing your reading speed using finger tracing

Try the following method:

- Select a reading passage of about two pages in length (you could use the sample text in Table 8.1). Note your starting and finishing time and calculate your reading speed using Method B in Table 8.2.
- Take a break of 40–60 minutes.
- Return to the text and run a finger along the line of text much faster than you could possibly read it.
- Repeat, but more slowly, so that you can just read it ('finger tracing'). Again, note your starting and finishing times, and work out your reading speed. You should find that your reading speed has increased from the first reading.
- Carry out this exercise at the same time of day over a week, using texts of similar length and complexity. This should help you to increase your reading speed through time.

Table 8.1 Sample reading text, showing reading 'signposts'. This text might represent the introduction to a textbook on modern communications in electrical engineering, journalism, marketing or psychology. The light shaded areas indicate the topic sentences; darker shading indicates the signpost words. You can also use this text of 744 words to assess your speed of reading (see Table 8.2).

Introduction Topic paragraph	Technological advances and skilful marketing have meant that the mobile phone has moved from being simply an accessory to a status as an essential piece of equipment. From teenagers to grandmothers, the nation has taken to the mobile phone as a constant link for business and social purposes. As a phenomenon, the ascendancy of the mobile phone, in a multitude of ways, has had a critical impact on the way people organise their lives.	Topic sentence
	Clearly, the convenience of the mobile is attractive. It is constantly available to receive or send calls. While these are not cheap, the less expensive text-message alternative provides a similar 'constant contact' facility. At a personal and social level, this brings peace of mind to parents as teenagers can locate and be located on the press of a button. However, in business terms, while it means that employees are constantly accessible and, with more sophisticated models, can access internet communications also, there is no escape from the workplace.	Signpost word Topic sentence Signpost word
	The emergence of abbreviated text-message language has wrought a change in everyday print. For example, pupils and students have been known to submit written work using text message symbols and language. Some have declared this to mark the demise of standard English. Furthermore, the accessibility of the mobile phone has become a problem in colleges and universities where it has been known for students in examinations to use the texting facility to obtain information required.	Topic sentence Signpost word Signpost word
	The ubiquity of the mobile phone has generated changes in the way that services are offered. For instance, this means that trains, buses, and restaurants have declared 'silent zones' where the mobile is not permitted, to give others a rest from the 'I'm on the train' style mobile phone conversation.	Topic sentence Signpost words
Transition paragraph	While the marked increase in mobile phone sales indicates that many in the population have embraced this technology, by contrast, 'mobile' culture has not been without its critics. Real concerns have been expressed about the potential dangers that can be encountered through mobile phone use.	Topic sentence Signpost words

Table 8.1 continued

	One such danger is that associated with driving while speaking on a mobile. A body of case law has been accumulated to support the introduction of new legislation outlawing the use of hand-held mobile phones by drivers while driving. The enforcement of this legislation is virtually impossible to police and, thus, much is down to the common sense and responsibility of drivers. Again, technology has risen to meet the contingency with the development of 'hands-free' phones that can be used while driving and without infringing the law.	Topic sentence Signpost word
	A further danger is an unseen one, namely the impact of the radiation from mobile phones on the human brain. Research is not well advanced in this area and data related to specific absorption rates (SARs) from the use of mobile phones and its effect on brain tissue is not yet available for evaluation. Nevertheless, although this lack of evidence is acknowledged by mobile phone companies, they advise that hands-free devices reduce the SARs levels by 98 per cent.	Topic sentence Signpost word
	Mobile phone controversy is not confined only to the potential dangers related to the units alone; some people have serious concerns about the impact mobile phone masts have on the area surrounding them. The fear is that radiation from masts could induce serious illness among those living near such masts. While evidence refuting or supporting this view remains inconclusive, there appears to be much more justification for concern about emissions from television transmitters and national grid pylons, which emit far higher levels of electro-magnetic radiation. Yet, little correlation appears to have been made between this fundamental of electrical engineering and the technology of telecommunications.	Topic sentence Signpost word Signpost word
Conclusion Terminator paragraph	In summary, although it appears that there are enormous benefits to mobile phone users, it is clear that there are many unanswered questions about the impact of their use on individuals. At one level, these represent an intrusion on personal privacy, whether as a user or as a bystander obliged to listen to multiple one-sided conversations in public places. More significantly, there is the potential for unseen damage to the health of individual users as they clamp their mobiles to their ears. Whereas the individual has a choice to use or not to use a mobile phone, people have fewer choices in relation to exposure to dangerous emissions from masts. While the output from phone masts is worthy of further investigation, it is in the more general context of emissions from electro-magnetic masts of all types that serious research needs to be developed.	Signpost words Topic sentence Signpost words Signpost word Signpost word

Table 8.2 **How to calculate your reading speed.** These two examples show the principles of how to do this calculation.

Method A (specified reading time)	
a Select a chapter from a textbook (this is better than a newspaper or journal because these are often printed in columns)	
b Calculate the average number of words per line, e.g. 50 words counted over 5 lines	= 10 words per line
c Count the number of lines per page	= 41 total lines
d Multiply (b × c) = 10 × 41	= 410 words per page
e Read for a specific time (to the nearest minute or half-minute) without stopping	= 4 minutes' reading
f Number of pages read in 4 minutes	= 2.5 pages read
g Multiply (d × f) = 410 × 2.5	= 1025 total words read
h Divide (g ÷ e) = 1025 ÷ 4	**= 256 words per minute**
Method B (specified text length)	
a Find a piece of text of known or estimated word length (see method A)	= 744 words
b Note the time taken to read this in seconds	= 170 seconds
c Convert the seconds to a decimal fraction of minutes = 170 ÷ 60	= 2.8 minutes
d Divide (a ÷ c) = 744 ÷ 2.8	**= 266 words per minute**

The average reading speed is said to be 265 words per minute (wpm). Reading speed for university students may be slightly lower, as aspects like difficulty of the text, unfamiliarity with the terminology used and the complexity of the concepts being discussed in the text have the potential to slow down reading. However, as you become more familiar with the subject and the issues being covered in your course and, thus, with your supplementary reading, then your reading speed will increase.

You can assess your normal reading speed using either method described in Table 8.2. The text of Table 8.1 is a suitable piece of writing whose word length is already known, should you wish to try method B. If your reading speed seems slow, then you can work on improving it by using a similar level and length of text at the same time each day. Go through the reading speed process and, gradually, you should see your average creeping up.

There are many other strategies you can develop to read and absorb content quickly. These include:

- **Skimming.** Pick out a specific piece of information by quickly letting your eye run down a list or over a page looking for a key word or phrase, as when seeking a particular name or address in a phone book.

- **Scanning.** Let your eye run quickly over a piece of text, for example, before you commit yourself to study-read the whole text. This will help you to gain an overview of the content before you start.

- **Picking out the topic sentences.** As seen above and in Figure 8.1 and Table 8.1, by reading the topic sentences you will be able to flesh out your overview of the text content. This will aid your understanding before you study-read the whole text.

- **Identifying the signpost words.** As noted above, these help guide you as the reader through the logical process that the author has mapped out for you.

- **Recognising clusters of grammatically allied words.** Subliminally, you will be grouping words in clusters according to their natural alliances. This will help you to read by making fewer fixations and this will improve your reading speed. You can improve your speed at doing this by using the eye-gymnastics exercise described earlier.

- **Taking cues from punctuation.** As you read, you will gain some understanding by interpreting the text using the cues of full stops and commas, for example, to help you gain understanding of what you are reading. The importance of punctuation to comprehension is vital (a point to remember as an academic author).

To be effective, reading quickly must be matched by a good level of comprehension, while reading too slowly can mean that comprehension is hampered. Clearly, you need to incorporate tests of your understanding to check that you have understood the main points of the text. One method of reading that incorporates this is called the SQ3R method – survey, question, read, recall and review (Table 8.3). This is also a helpful strategy for exam revision as it incorporates the development of memory and learning skills simultaneously. Another test of assimilation is note-making. This is covered in **Ch 10**.

Table 8.3 **Reading for remembering: the SQ3R method.** The point of this method is that the reader has to engage in processing the material in the text and is not simply reading on 'autopilot' where very little is being retained.

Survey stage
• Read the first paragraph (topic paragraph) and last paragraph (terminator paragraph) of a chapter or page of notes • Read the intervening paragraph topic sentences • Focus on the headings and sub-headings, if present • Study the graphs and diagrams for key features
Question stage
• What do you know already about this topic? • What is the author likely to tell you? • What specifically do you need to find out?
Read stage
• Read the entire section *quickly* to get the gist of the piece of writing; finger-tracing techniques may be helpful at this point • Go back to the question stage and revisit your initial answers • Look especially for keywords, key statements, signpost words • Do *not* stop to look up unknown words – go for completion
Recall stage
• Turn the book or your notes over and try to recall as much as possible • Make key pattern headings/notes/diagrams/flow charts (Ch 10) • Turn over the book again • Check over for accuracy of recall; suggested recall periods – every 20 minutes
Review stage
• After a break, try to recall the main points

Practical tips for reading effectively and with understanding

Be selective and understand your purpose. Think about why you are reading. Look at the material you have already collected relating to the subject or topic you aim to research. For example, this may even include lecture notes, which ought to remind you of the way a particular topic was presented, the thrust of an argument or a procedure. Are you reading to obtain a general overview or is it to identify additional specific information? Use a technique and material that suits your needs.

Adjust your reading speed according to the type of text you have to read. For example, a marginally interesting article in a general publication will probably require less intensive reading than a key chapter in an academic book or an article from an academic journal.

Grasp the general message before dealing with difficult parts. Not all academic printed material is 'reader friendly'. If you find a section of text difficult to understand, then skip over that bit; toiling over it will not increase your understanding. Continue with your reading and when you come to a natural break in the text, for example, the end of a chapter or section, then go back to the 'sticky' bit and re-read it. Usually, second time round, it will make more sense because you have an overview of the context. Similarly, don't stop every time you come across a new word. Read on and try to get the gist of the meaning from the rest of the text. When you have finished, look the word up in a dictionary and add to your personal glossary.

Take regular breaks. Reading continuously over a long period of time is counterproductive. Concentration is at a peak after 20 minutes, but wanes after 40 minutes. Take regular breaks, making sure that your breaks do not become longer than your study periods.

Follow up references within your text. When you are reading, you need to be conscious of the citations to other authors that might be given in the text; not all will be relevant to your reading purpose, but it is worth quickly noting the ones that look most interesting as you come across them. You'll usually find the full publication details in the references at the end of the chapter/article or at the end of the book. This will give you sufficient information to access supplementary reading once you have finished reading the 'parent' text.

 **And now . . .**

8.1 **Monitor your reading speed.** Choose a suitable text and calculate your speed using either method A or B in Table 8.2. If you feel your speed is relatively slow, then try out some of the methods suggested in the speed-reading section of this chapter. After a spell of using these methods, and having decided which suit you, check your speed to see if you have improved.

▶

8.2 Practise surveying a text. Rather than simply opening your reading resource at the pages that appear to be most relevant, spend a few minutes surveying the whole paper or book. Think about how the author has organised the content and why. Keep this in mind when reading the text, and reflect on whether this has improved your comprehension and assimilation of the content. As a bonus your quick survey may reveal more relevant information that you might otherwise have missed.

8.3 Become more familiar with the visual reading cues embedded within texts. Conventions of grammar, punctuation and spelling are useful in providing clues to meaning for the reader (see Table 8.1, for example). If you would like to look into these topics further, then see **Ch 22**.

Time management

How to balance study, family, work and leisure

Managing your time effectively is an important key to a fulfilling university career. This chapter provides ideas for organising your activities and tips to help you focus on important tasks.

Key topics:
→ Diaries, timetables and planners
→ Listing and prioritising
→ Routines and good work habits
→ How to avoid putting things off

Key terms
Perfectionism   Prioritising   Writer's block

Successful people tend to have the ability to focus on the right tasks at the right time, the capacity to work quickly to meet their targets, and the knack of seeing each job through to a conclusion. In short, they possess good time-management skills. Time management is a skill that can be developed like any other. Here are some simple routines and tips that can help you improve your organisation, prioritisation and time-keeping. Weigh up the following ideas and try to adopt those most suited to your needs and personality.

As a student, you will need to balance the time you devote to study, family, work and social activities. Although you probably have more freedom over these choices than many others, making the necessary decisions is still a challenging task. Table 8.1 demonstrates just how easy it is for students' study time to evaporate.

→ Diaries, timetables and planners

Organising your activities more methodically is an obvious way to gain useful time.

Diaries and student planners

Use a diary or planner to keep track of your day-to-day schedule (for example, lectures, sports activities) and to note submission deadlines for university work.

- Work your way back from key dates, creating milestones such as 'finish library work for essay' or 'prepare first draft of essay'.
- Refer to the diary or planner frequently to keep yourself on track and to plan out each day and week. Try to get into the habit of looking at the next day's activities the night before and the next week's work at the end of the week. If you use a diary

From Chapter 8 of *The Smarter Study Skills Companion*, 2/e. Kathleen McMillan. Jonathan Weyers. © Pearson Education Limited 2006, 2009. All rights reserved.

Table 8.1 **Some of the ways in which students' study time evaporates.** Do you recognise any of these traits in yourself?

Personality type	Typical working ways . . . and the problems that may result
The late-nighter	Luke likes to work into the small hours. He's got an essay to write with a deadline tomorrow morning, but just couldn't get down to doing it earlier on. It's 2.00 a.m. and now he's panicking. Because the library's shut, he can't find a reference to support one of his points; he's so tired he won't be able to review his writing and correct the punctuation and grammatical errors; and he feels so shattered that he'll probably sleep in and miss the 9.00 a.m. deadline. Oh well, the essay was only worth 25 per cent – he'll just have to make up the lost marks in the exam . . .
The extension-seeker	Eleanor always rationalises being late with her assignments. She always has good reasons for being late, and it's never her fault. This is beginning to wear rather thin with her tutors. This time her printer packed up just before submission, last time she had tonsillitis and the time before she had to visit her granny in hospital. She's asked for an extension, but will lose 10 per cent of the marks for every day her work is late. It's only a small amount, but as she's a borderline pass in this subject, it could make all the difference . . .
The stressed-out non-starter	Shahid has to give a presentation to his tutorial group. Only thing is, he's so intimidated by the thought of standing up in front of them, that he can't focus on writing the talk. If only he had his PowerPoint slides and notes ready, he'd feel a whole lot more confident about things, but he can't get going because of his nerves. Maybe if he just goes out for a walk, he'll feel better placed to start when he comes back . . . and then, maybe another cup of coffee . . .
The last-minuter	Lorna is a last-minute person and she can only get motivated when things get close to the wire. She produces her best work close to deadlines when the adrenaline is flowing. However, her final-year dissertation is supposed to be a massive 10,000 words, there's only a week to go and she hasn't felt nervous enough to get started until now . . .
The know-it-all	Ken has it all under control. The lecture notes are all on the Web, so there's really no need to go to the lectures. He'll catch up on sleep instead and study by himself later on. Then he'll just stroll into the exam looking cool, get stuck in and amaze everyone with his results. Trouble is, the professor gave out a sheet changing the learning outcomes at her first lecture, missed out one of the topics (which Ken has revised carefully) and told the other students that the exam format now involves two compulsory questions . . .
The perfectionist	Pat wants to do really well at uni. She signed up for a vocational degree and has plans to land a plum job on graduation to start her climb up the career tree. Mum and Dad want her to do really well in her assignments and it's vital that the essay that she's working on starts with a cracking first sentence. Just can't phrase it right though – she's tried 15 different ways and crossed them all out. Time is running out now, and she will have to put off going to the Globetrotter's Dance. Well, who needs a social life anyway . . .
The juggler	Jeff is a mature student and is working part-time to make ends meet. Although it started as 10 hours a week, it's now up to 25. He's juggling his shifts so he can attend lectures and tutorials, and might be able to do a bit of coursework in the breaks at work, providing the staffroom is empty. He can't get into the library to work on the short-loan material, so he'll have to miss that out. And he's so tired at the end of each day, he just can't summon the energy to read the core texts. Doesn't know how long he can keep this pace up . . .

with the 'week-to-view' type of layout, you will be able to see ahead each time you look at it.

- Number the weeks, so you can sense how time is progressing over longer periods, such as a term or semester.
- Consider also numbering the weeks in reverse 'count down' fashion to key events such as end of semester/term exams and assignment submission dates.

Choosing a diary or planner

Some universities and many bookshops sell academic diaries that cover the year from September to August. Alternatively, some sell academic planners, such as *The Smarter Student Planner*, which provide templates for planning that allow you to keep track of assignment dates, plan for exam revision as well as providing reviews of key points of grammar, spelling, punctuation and maths.

Timetables

Create a detailed timetable of study when you have a big task looming (e.g. before exams, or when there is a large report or literature survey to write up). The use of revision timetables is covered further in **Ch 64**, and the same principles apply to other tasks. You could:

- break the task down into smaller parts;
- space these out appropriately;
- schedule important activities for when you generally feel most intellectually active (e.g. mid-morning).

One advantage of a timetable is that you can see the progress you are making if you cross out or highlight each mini-task as it is completed.

Wall planners

These are another way of charting out your activities, with the advantage, like a timetable, that you can see everything in front of you.

Advantages of being organised

If you organise your time well, you will:

- keep on schedule and meet deadlines;
- reduce stress caused by a feeling of lack of control over your work schedule;
- complete work with less pressure and fulfil your potential;
- build your confidence about your ability to cope;
- avoid overlapping assignments and having to juggle more than one piece of work at a time.

Being organised is especially important for large or long-term tasks because it seems easier to put things off when deadlines seem a long way off.

→ Listing and prioritising

At times you may run into problems because you have a number of different tasks that need to be done. It is much better to write these tasks down in a list each day, rather than risk forgetting them. You will then have a good picture of what needs to be done and will be better able to prioritise the tasks.

High ← Urgency ← Low

Low → Importance → High

1	2
3	4

Figure 8.1 **The urgent-important approach to prioritising.** Place each activity somewhere on the axes in relation to its importance and urgency. Do all the activities in sector 1 first, then 2 or 3, and last 4.

Once you've created a list, rank the tasks by numbering them from 1, 2, 3 and so on, in order from 'important and urgent' to 'neither important nor urgent' (see Figure 8.1). Your 'important' criteria will depend on many factors: for example, your own goals, the weight of marks given to each assessment, or how far away the submission date is.

Each day, you should try to complete as many of the listed tasks as you can, starting with number one. If you keep each day's list achievable, the process of striking out each task as it is completed provides a feeling of progress being made, which turns into one of satisfaction if the list has virtually disappeared by the evening. Also, you will become less stressed once high-priority tasks are tackled.

Carry over any uncompleted tasks to the next day, add new ones to your list and start again – but try to complete yesterday's unfinished jobs before starting new ones of similar priority, or they will end up being delayed for too long.

Deciding on priorities

This involves distinguishing between important and urgent activities.

- **Importance** implies some assessment of the benefits of completing a task against the loss if the task is not finished.
- **Urgency** relates to the length of time before the task must be completed.

For example, in normal circumstances, doing your laundry will be neither terribly important nor particularly urgent, but if you start to run out of clean underwear, you may decide otherwise. Hence, priorities are not static and need to be reassessed frequently.

→ Routines and good work habits

Many people find that carrying out specific tasks at special periods of the day or times of the week helps them get things accomplished on time. You may already adopt this approach with routine tasks like doing your laundry every Tuesday morning or visiting a relative on Sunday afternoons. You may find it helps to add work-related activities to your list of routines – for example, by making Monday evening a time for library study, working on whatever assignment is next on your list.

Good working habits can help with time management:

- **Do important work when you are at your most productive.** Most of us can state when we work best (Figure 8.2). When you have worked this out for yourself, timetable your activities to suit: academic work when you are 'most awake' and routine activities when you are less alert.
- **Make the most of small scraps of time.** Use otherwise unproductive time, such as when commuting or before going to sleep, to jot down ideas, edit work or make plans. Keep a notebook with you to write down your thoughts.
- **Keep your documents organised.** If your papers are well filed, you won't waste time looking for something required for the next step.
- **Make sure you always have a plan.** Often, the reason projects don't go well is because there is no scheme to work to. Laying out a plan for an essay, report or project helps you to clarify the likely structure behind your efforts. Writing out a fairly detailed plan will save you time in the long run.
- **Extend your working day.** If you can deal with early rising, you may find that setting your alarm earlier than normal provides a few extra minutes or hours to help you achieve a short-term goal.

Time period	Alertness rating
am	
pm	
pm	
pm/am	

Figure 8.2 **Are you a morning, afternoon, evening or night person?** Rate yourself (marks out of 10) according to when you find yourself most alert and able to study productively.

→ How to avoid putting things off

One of the hardest parts of time management is getting started on tasks. Procrastination is all too easy, and can involve the following:

- convincing yourself that other low-priority work is more important or preferable;
- switching frequently among tasks, and not making much progress in any of them;
- talking about your work rather than doing it;
- planning for too long rather than working;
- having difficulty starting a piece of writing (having 'writer's block');
- spending too long on presentational elements (e.g. the cover page or a diagram), rather than the 'meat' of the project.

Definition: procrastination

This is simply putting off a task for another occasion. As the poet, Edward Young, wrote: 'Procrastination is the thief of time'.

A particular type of procrastination involves displacement activity – doing things that help you to avoid a difficult or distasteful task. For example:

- Do you really need to check and answer all your texts and emails before getting down to work?
- Do you really need to watch that TV programme or have another spell at that computer game?
- Why are you cooking tonight, rather than eating fast food and getting down to your studies much quicker?
- Why are you drawing such a neat diagram, when creating a less tidy one will let you get on to the next topic?
- Why are you so keen to chat to your friends rather than go to the library?
- Why are you shopping today, when you could easily leave it until later?

The first step in preventing the syndrome of procrastination, and especially displacement activity, is to recognise what your subconscious is doing. You need to make a conscious effort to counteract this side of your personality, by analysing your behaviour and possibly setting yourself time or other targets with 'rewards' to tempt you into meeting these. For example, 'I'll take a break when I've written the next section, 200 words . . .'

You might also make a list of things that need to be done and prioritise these into 'immediate', 'soon' and 'later' categories. Convince yourself that you will not start on the 'soon' and 'later' categories until you have fulfilled all those items on the 'immediate' list. And don't be tempted to think that if you get the smaller things out of the way that will free up your mind for the bigger issues – all that will happen is that more lower-category issues will creep into your attention.

Delaying completion of a task, in itself a form of procrastination, is another aspect of time management that many find difficult. It's a special problem for those afflicted by perfectionism. Good time managers recognise when to finish tasks, even if the task is not in a 'perfect' state. At university, doing this can mean that the sum of results from multiple assignments is better, because your attention is divided more appropriately, rather than focusing on a single task at the expense of others.

Tips for getting started on tasks and completing them on time are provided in Table 8.2.

Table 8.2 Ten tips for getting started on academic tasks and completing them on time

1 **Improve your study environment.** Your focus and concentration will depend on this. • Create a tidy workplace. Although tidying up can be a symptom of procrastination, in general it is easier to start studying at an empty desk and in an uncluttered room. • Reduce noise. Some like background music, while others don't – but it's generally other people's noise that really interrupts your train of thought. A solution might be to go to a quiet place like a library. • Escape. Why not take all you need to a different location where there will be a minimum of interruptions? Your focus will be enhanced if the task you need to do is the only thing you can do, so take with you only the notes and papers you require.
2 **Avoid distractions.** If you are easily tempted away from tasks by your friends, you'll have to learn to decline their invitations politely. Hang up a 'do not disturb' sign, and explain why to your friends; disappear off to a quieter location without telling anyone where you will be; or switch off your phone, TV or email program. One strategy might be to say to friends, 'I can't come just now, but how about having a short break in half an hour?'
3 **Work in short bursts while your concentration is at a maximum.** After this, give yourself a brief break, perhaps by going for a short walk, and then start back again.
4 **Find a way to start.** Breaking initial barriers is vital. When writing, this is a very common problem because of the perceived need to begin with a 'high impact' sentence that reads impressively. This is unnecessary, and starting with a simple definition or restatement of the question or problem is perfectly acceptable. If you lack the motivation to begin work, try thinking briefly about the bigger picture: your degree and career, and how the current task is a small but essential step to achieving your goals.
5 **Focus on the positive.** You may be so anxious about the end point of your task that this affects your ability to start it. For example, many students are so nervous about exams or speaking in public that they freeze in their preparation and put the whole thing off. One way to counter this would be to practise – perhaps through mock exams or rehearsing an oral presentation with a friend. Focus on positive aspects – things you do know, rather than those you don't; or the good results you want to tell people about, rather than those that failed to provide answers.
6 **In written tasks, don't feel you have to work in a linear fashion.** Word-processing software allows you work out of sequence, which can help get you going. So, for a large report, it might help to start on a part that is 'mechanical', such as a reference list or results section. Sometimes it's a good idea to draft the summary, abstract or contents list first, because this will give you a plan to work to.
7 **Cut up large tasks.** If you feel overwhelmed by the size of a job and this prevents you from starting it, break the task down to manageable, achievable chunks. Then, try to complete something every day. Maintaining momentum in this way will allow you to whittle away the job in small pieces.
8 **Work alongside others.** If you arrange to work alongside others, you can spur each other on with sympathy, humour and the promise of a drink or coffee after each study period.
9 **Ask for help.** You may feel that you lack a particular skill to attempt some component of the task (e.g. maths, spelling, or the ability to use a software program) and that this is holding you back. Don't be afraid to ask for help. Rather than suffering in isolation, consult a fellow student, lecturer, or skills adviser; or visit one of the many websites that offer assistance.
10 **Don't be too much of a perfectionist.** We all want to do well, but doing your very best takes time – a commodity that should be carefully rationed so that all tasks are given their fair share. Perfectionism can prevent or delay you getting started if you feel your initial efforts need to be faultless (see 4 above). Also, achieving fault-free work requires progressively more effort, with less return as you get nearer to perfection. The time you need to spend to attain the highest standards will probably be better used on the next task.

Practical tips for managing your time

Invest in items to support your time management. Helpful items could include a diary, wall planner, personal digital assistant (PDA), mobile phone with diary facility, and alarm clock – then use them!

Investigate how you really use your time. Time-management experts often ask clients to write down what they do for every minute of several days and thereby work out where the productive time disappears to. If you are unsure exactly what you waste time on, you might like to keep a detailed record for a short period, using a suitable coding for your activities. When you have identified the time-wasting aspects of your day, you can then act to cut these down (or out). Those of a more numerical bent might wish to construct a spreadsheet to do this and work out percentages spent on different activities. Once you have completed your timesheet, analyse it to see whether you spend excessive amounts of time on any one activity or may not have the balance right. As you think about this, remember that universities assume you will be carrying out academic-related activities for roughly 40 hours per week.

Create artificial deadlines. Set yourself a finishing date that is ahead of the formal submission deadline for your assignment. That way you will have the time to review your work, correct errors and improve the quality of presentation.

Build flexibility into your planning. We often end up rushing things because the unexpected has interrupted a timetable that is too tightly scheduled. To avoid this, deliberately introduce empty slots into your plans to allow for these contingencies.

Try to prioritise the items on your 'to do' list. If you produce a daily list of tasks, spend some time thinking about how you wish to prioritise and order them through the day. You might adopt a numerical system or one using stars, for example.

Ask yourself whether your lifestyle needs radical surgery. You may find that little in this chapter seems relevant because your time is dominated by a single activity. This might be socialising, caring for others, outside employment or travelling, for example. In these cases, you may need to make fundamental changes to your lifestyle to place greater emphasis on your studies. In some cases a student counsellor might be able to help you decide what needs to be done.

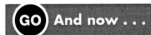 **And now . . .**

8.1 Analyse your time-management personality. Read through this chapter and particularly Table 8.1. Can you recognise any character traits that are preventing you from organising your time effectively? Might any of the 'Practical tips' help you become better at time management? How could you adapt them to your own situation?

8.2 Experiment with listing and prioritising. If you haven't used this method before, test it out for a week or so. Make a list of all your current and future tasks, assignments, appointments and social events. If they are large, subdivide them into smaller components. Rearrange the list in order of priority. Take special care to take account of events that depend on other jobs being completed. Now try to complete the different components, ticking them off the list as you go. After your trial period, decide how effective the method was in organising your activities and helping you to ensure that tasks were done on time.

8.3 Declutter and reorganise your life. If you reckon disorganisation is a reason for lack of progress (Table 8.2), make a determined effort to tidy things up. Start with your room and study environment, and if necessary invest in files and boxes to help you organise things. Keep out only that which is relevant to current activities and carefully store the rest. Decide how you can better arrange your affairs to keep on top of routine tasks. Now you should be in a better mental and physical position to get started on your next assignment.

Libraries are more than collections of books

When you choose your various courses, you'll be given reading lists of recommended texts. But they're just part of the written word resources you'll need. Remember we stressed that, in this new learning environment, you're independent and have to take responsibility for your own choices. So you'll be expected to locate additional material for yourself, which means developing the skills to recognise where the gaps in your reading are and how to plug them.

How to use the library

You might be thinking this is an unnecessary chapter. After all, we all know what libraries are and what you do in them. You go there, borrow a book, and that's it. Maybe, but university libraries are much more than collections of books and journals. For students, they're a major resource with information in many forms. As well as the items they carry on their shelves, they represent electronic gateways to a massive amount of online information. With so much material at your fingertips and such specific topics to research, you need to know how to focus on what's available, what's relevant and how to access it in its most useful forms.

Join the library

The first, obvious step is to make sure you're a member with borrowing rights. So, once you've matriculated, find the university library and activate your membership. Register for one of the tours which the librarians organise. They'll take you round, identify the places and facilities that are available, and you can ask them questions. While you're there, check out any leaflets or maps which you can use later when you're finding your own way round.

The moment you join, you're on the library system and there's a record established in your name. It's usually done electronically and you'll be able to check which books you've borrowed, which are due for return and other relevant information.

More than books

As well as books, most university libraries have copies of some newspapers, periodicals and academic journals. There'll be many kinds of reference materials, perhaps slides, photographs, videos and DVDs. There'll also be areas set aside for particular types of study. The most obvious are the quiet study areas, but there may also be places for group work where you're allowed to discuss things. Photocopiers and printers will probably be available, along with computing terminals and possibly a wireless network. You'll have access to online catalogues and, of course, the library staff are there to support you, either in person or through the library website. So there's definitely more than books.

The materials (including books) that are carried will depend on what degrees are being taught, any teaching specialisms, the research interests of staff and what collections may have been left to the university. Each library is unique and you may find archive materials that aren't available anywhere else.

brilliant tip

Some reading lists are long and the books on them are expensive. If you need to refer to a particular book frequently and/or it relates closely to your lectures and coursework, it's obviously worth buying your own copy. But if not, check to see if it's in the library and how many copies they carry. (You may have problems if all the other students in your class need to consult the same thing at the same time.)

Digital and web-based resources

Today, vast amounts of material are accessible online in just about every area of interest. Libraries have subscriptions to e-book repositories, e-journals, e-newspapers and online dictionaries and encyclopaedias. Your institution will have its dedicated system of letting you access these digitised and web-based resources and you'll probably need a password. It'll pay you to get to know the details of your system as early as possible. These are resources that are available 24/7 from any computer connected to the internet. They may also allow more than one person to access an e-book at the same time. Some e-book facilities, such as ebrary, have extra tools which let you search, make notes and consult linked online dictionaries to check the meanings of words.

There are now many electronic databases which make it easier to get access to information from public bodies, and most of them are available online. For example, you can look at statistical population details on the National Statistics website (www.statistics.gov.uk), and any papers and publications produced by the Houses of Parliament at www.parliament. uk. Access to academic journals and other material will depend on whether your library subscribes to them or not, so find out which search engines and databases are available to you.

Paper-based resources

The most obvious of these are the books:

- Your prescribed texts link with the content of your courses.
- General textbooks provide a broader overview of the subject.
- Supplementary texts discuss topics in greater depth.

Then come the many different kinds of reference books:

- Standard dictionaries help with spelling, pronunciation and meaning.
- Bilingual dictionaries translate words and expressions in two languages.
- Subject-specific dictionaries define important terms relating to a particular discipline.

- Thesauri (which is the plural form of thesaurus) give you synonyms, i.e. words similar in meaning to the one you're looking up. A–Z versions are easier to use than the original *Roget's Thesaurus*.

- General encyclopaedias provide a quick overview of or introduction to a new topic.

- Discipline-specific encyclopaedias have in-depth coverage of specific topics.

- Biographical dictionaries and other material are excellent sources of information on both contemporary and historical figures.

- Yearbooks and directories carry up-to-date information on organisations.

- Atlases provide geographical and historical information.

Finally, there are newspapers and journals:

- Newspapers, both daily and weekly, cover contemporary issues.

- Periodicals and academic journals are publications which are specific to a particular discipline or subject. They usually appear three or four times a year and provide new ideas, reports and comment on current research issues.

- Popular periodicals such as *Nature, New Scientist* and *The Economist* deal with broader issues and emerging trends in the fields of study indicated by their titles.

Shared library resources

Many university libraries share resources with those of neighbouring institutions. They're all linked to the British Library too, which is the national library of the UK. This receives a copy of every publication produced in the UK and Ireland, and its massive collection of over 150 million items increases by 3 million every year. Some university libraries are known as European Documentation Centres (http://ec.europa.eu/europedirect). They hold important documents of the European Union.

Getting to know the system

You'll have plenty to be thinking about without having to worry whether books are on the shelves, overdue, on short- or long-term loans and all the rest of it, so find out the rules you need to know as a borrower.

🅿️ brilliant questions and answers

Q How many books can I borrow at any one time?

A That depends on your status. Staff and postgraduate students can usually borrow more books than undergraduates.

Q How long can I keep the item I've borrowed?

A It depends on what it is. Normal loans are usually for several weeks. But there may be a big demand for some books because they're prescribed texts, so they may be put on a short-loan system. That means you can take them out but have to hand them back earlier than with 'normal' books – maybe in a matter of a few hours, but usually it's a few days.

Q What's the fine if I keep it longer than I'm supposed to?

A It depends on the sort of book. If it's a short-term loan, the fine will be higher than 'normal' loans. It may just be a few pence, but think about it. If you've got ten books you should have handed back two weeks ago, that'll cost you £10 or more.

Q How can I renew the loan?

A By phone with most libraries and, more and more, online. Check your university's home page.

Electronic book tagging

Most universities operate a system of electronic 'book tagging' to make sure that resources can't be taken out without being logged out to a particular user. This means that all books need to be 'de-activated' before you can take them outside the library.

Regulations and codes of conduct

You'll see notices on leaflets and websites telling or reminding you of the library rules. They're important because they're there to protect the resources and also regulate the studying environment for you and all the other users, asking you to be aware of the needs of others studying around you. In particular, they spell out your legal responsibilities under copyright law and tell you how much you can photocopy from a specific book or document.

brilliant tip

If your library uses a card system for photocopying, write your name and a contact number on the card they issue to you. It's all too easy to leave it on a machine.

Information literacy skills

What's information literacy? Well, it's all about realising you need information and knowing where to find it and how to use it. It may sound pretty basic, but there are more steps in the process than you might think at first. You need to be able to:

- recognise that you need a piece of information
- think of ways to plug that gap
- decide how you're going to find and access the information
- compare and evaluate information you get from different sources
- organise, apply and communicate information to others according to what's required of you
- synthesise and build upon existing information to help expand it and create new knowledge.

It's worth taking a moment to think about these different stages, recognise the differences between them and ask yourself how competent you are at each of them. To help you answer that question, consider some of the basic skills you'll need to master.

- You'll need to be familiar with how electronic catalogues work in order not to waste time in fruitless searches. Most let you search by author, title or subject, but there may be other alternatives on your system.

● When you identify the book that you want from the catalogue, you'll want to know which shelf it's on. So you need to take a note of two things: the location (because the book might even be in another site library) and the number, which may be a sequence of letters and/or numbers depending on the system your library uses. It's on the spine of the book and books are all arranged in sequence in stacks. At the end of each stack you'll find the numbers of the first and last books in the sequence they contain. If you can't find what you're looking for, library staff will help you.

● Sometimes a book may not be available in your own library and you may want to borrow it from another UK library. There's usually a librarian who's responsible for inter-library loans so that's the person you need to consult. Be careful, though, as there's usually a fee to pay for this and you're the one who has to pay it.

● We spoke earlier of the various e-resources you might use. Normally, you'll access them through the library's website. Some are open-access, but for others you'll need a password so that publishers can check that your library has subscribed to a particular resource and that you have access rights. Systems vary, but usually there'll be special training sessions in lectures or arranged independently in the library. There's a wealth of material; don't be fazed by it. Ask a librarian to help you find your way around it all.

brilliant tip

Imagine your lecturer has mentioned an article by someone called Nichol which you should read. You look up the name, but there's no sign of the article. That may be because she may be called Nicol, Nicoll, Nickol or many other variations of the surname. So, if you haven't seen a name written down (in your course handbook, for example), try different options to get the one you want.

Look further afield

Find and join the local public library. It may have some texts relevant to your course and they won't be in such heavy demand as those in the university library. Some university libraries have agreements with other, similar ones in the area, including national libraries. This obviously extends the resources available to you and you should take advantage of such arrangements. You can use the facilities and sometimes even borrow books from partner libraries.

Explore all the library locations available to you. You may find some with different study areas that are more convenient or that suit your moods, learning preference or personality. You may prefer peace and quiet or work better if there's some activity around you as you study.

And make sure you know about all the alternative library facilities on your campus. There may be satellite libraries on different parts of the site or in different buildings. Some of these may be departmental libraries with specialist resources. They may also hold duplicates of books in the main library.

Of course, finding information on the shelves and online is only the first step. It's important to know how best to use it for your studies. Next you need to evaluate it and use it appropriately in your academic writing, note-making and revision. The reason we mention this here is that it helps enormously if, when you find the information you need, you note the details of where you found it. We'll deal with how to do that later, but it's never too early to point out that plagiarism is theft. So, if you use material from a specific book, article or other publication, always acknowledge where it came from and who wrote it.

---

brilliant example

There are two main cataloguing systems; the one your library uses will be explained in leaflets or during the library tour.

The two systems are:

- the Dewey decimal system, in which each book is given a number. For example, editions of Shakespeare's *Hamlet* are filed under 822.33
- the Library of Congress system, which uses an alphanumeric code, so the same editions of *Hamlet* would be filed under PR2807.

There may be small variations in how these are interpreted, so the important thing is to find out exactly how your own library's system works.

What next?

Try to go on a library tour ...

... and if you see or hear things you don't understand, ask about them. In many ways university libraries are different from public libraries and they've got much more to offer. If your university doesn't organise tours, see if you can take a virtual tour through your university library's website.

Get to know the electronic library resources ...

... particularly any which are specific to your own subjects, and explore the shelves covering your subject area. Find this area by looking in the library catalogue and the information on the book stacks. When you do, browse through what's there. You may find interesting books and catalogues which you might not have come across otherwise.

When you find something in a book ...

... which isn't on your list of recommended reading, make sure it's a reliable source. Check that it's by someone qualified to write about the subject, with good academic credentials, and that it's not out of date.

 recap

The range of facilities and resources.

Getting to know the system.

Regulations and codes of conduct.

Information literacy skills.

Looking further afield.

LOCATING SOURCES

This chapter stresses the importance of searching for sources systematically and invites you to consider the relevance, ready availability, and reliability of materials in relation to your topic. It also provides tips on effective time management as you search the literature in your subject area.

The chapter covers:

- Systematic searching for sources
- The relevance of sources
- The ready availability of sources
- The reliability of sources
- Literature searches
- Using your university library
- Moving from general to specific research.

Using this chapter

From Chapter 3 of *Academic Research, Writing & Referencing*, 1/e. Mary deane.
© Pearson Education Limited 2010. All rights reserved.

INTRODUCTION

Chapter 2 offered tips on avoiding plagiarism; Chapter 3 now highlights the need for a system to search for the sources you will use in your writing. It stresses the importance of understanding your purpose for writing and explains how to move from seeking general sources to finding specifically relevant materials.

A SYSTEM FOR SEARCHING

Although your approach will differ based on the purpose of each writing task, you can develop a system for locating potentially useful sources that is adaptable to each assignment (Hacker 2006: 6, Lunsford 2008: 258).

Sources should be:

■ Relevant
■ Readily available
■ Reliable.

Relevance

The relevance of sources depends upon the content, style, author, and intended audience (Lunsford 2008: 252). The clearer you are about the aim, style, and format of your own work, the better equipped you will be to find the right kinds of texts for your purpose. Do not neglect to search for numerical data and images if these are also relevant. Begin your systematic approach to locating the right sources for your task by thinking about these three questions:

1 What is the scope of the source?
2 Is this relevant to my writing?
3 Should I just make a record of this source (using a referencing management system, on paper, or on file) and move on?

Readily available

Once you have learnt how to use the catalogue, databases, and resources readily available via your university library you will not be dependent upon the internet, which is only one way to access materials and will not necessarily yield relevant sources for your purpose (Hacker 2006: 10). The next phase in your systematic approach to searching for sources is to consider these three questions:

1 Is there a paper-based copy in my university library?
2 Do I need to order the source from another library or collection?
3 Is there a digital copy accessible via my university library website using the catalogue, databases, or search engines?

Reliability

Sources are reliable if they are accurate, well designed, and written by authors with the right credentials for your purpose (Hacker 2006: 23). Mostly you will need to refer to scholarly sources for your academic writing, so the material you select should be based on valid research. It is often preferable to consult peer-reviewed sources because they have been verified by experts in the field. The third stage in your systematic approach to searching is to address these questions:

1 Is the information in the source confirmed elsewhere?
2 Is the author qualified to produce the source?
3 Is the source intended for academic use?

Peer review

Peer review is a process designed to ensure the quality, reliability, and originality of published material. Tutors often expect you to locate sources that have been peer-reviewed, which means that expert readers evaluate material and provide feedback on the areas requiring improvement, expansion, or revision. Blind peer review is when feedback is supplied anonymously and this is considered to be a more rigorous form of assessment.

If you are not sure whether sources have been peer-reviewed you can ask for advice at your university library or consult your tutors. The challenge of accessing sources online is that sources distributed via this digital environment do not always undergo peer review, and consequently they can be poorly phrased, badly organised or inaccurate. Therefore, do not rely exclusively on sources you have accessed online and instead research scholarly materials which have been assessed by experts and identified as reliable for academic use (Hacker 2006: 24–6).

RELEVANT SOURCES

When you receive an assignment brief or writing project, one of your first tasks is to analyse the requirements and begin to search for sources to help you fulfil your brief. It is often necessary to do independent research, and most often you will not be able to carry out the task successfully without drawing on existing knowledge. As discussed in the next chapter, your use of sources must be documented fully to avoid unintentional plagiarism.

Researching existing ideas can help you to formulate your own perspective on a subject, which will contribute to making your academic writing original. In most contexts this quality is highly valued, so enhancing the innovative nature of your work could improve your performance. However, originality is an often misunderstood term and is not as demanding as it may appear because, although your tutors expect a fresh engagement with topics from each student, they are aware of the constraints of time and experience. So, in practice and especially at undergraduate level, originality is achieved mainly through original research, which helps writers identify fresh angles on their topics.

Researching existing ideas can also give you the authority to deal with a subject effectively, because the more you know about a topic the more confident your treatment of it will be. Writers who are unclear about important issues are unlikely to organise their material well, which will have a negative impact on the quality of their writing. If you have a strong understanding of a particular topic you will be in the best position to identify the most cogent points to include or debate, which means that you will not include irrelevant data which disrupts the flow of ideas. Effective research will help you to gain clarity about the ideas and information you are discussing – this can improve your written expression to create an impression of professionalism and mastery of your material.

Keep focused on your deadline

Whilst research is usually essential to effective academic writing it is also vital to limit the time you spend locating sources so that you can maximise the time available for assessing, reading critically, and integrating sources into your assignments. The three-stage process outlined below offers tips on being efficient and effective as you gather information before you start to write. However, this is just one approach to research and you should adapt it to suit your own style as a scholar.

Collect together all the guidance you have received from your tutor about producing your piece of writing. This may include the assignment brief, the module handbook, and notes from lectures or seminars. Tutors often put coursework guidelines on the module web, so, if relevant, have a look at this. The earlier you gather these guidelines, the better your chances will be of getting support about issues you do not understand.

Here are five important questions to ask yourself when you are analysing the purpose of your writing in order to locate appropriate sources:

1 Who is the main audience for this piece of writing? (For instance, subject specialists)
2 What information should I assume this readership already knows? (I will not need to explain this in my writing)
3 What do I already know? (From lecture notes, readings, experience)
4 What background information do I need to acquire? (This should be presented in a concise way early in my writing)
5 Which key terms, concepts, or theories do I need to research? (Do I need advice about these?)

Find the right sources for your purpose

Jot down your answers to these five questions and take your notes to the library when you go to research or keep them with you as you go online to find appropriate

46

databases via the library website. The advantage of visiting the library in person is that you may be able to speak to a library specialist on duty, who can help you to locate the best sources for your purpose.

Work with others to find suitable sources

Discuss the kinds of sources you might use with others who are studying your subject, either by chatting in person or corresponding online. Although it would be plagiarism to copy another person's work, it is good practice to search for information together, as long as you generate your own ideas for writing about the sources you find.

You could develop a joint plan for locating sources with a friend and divide the task between you; for example, if you need to investigate several theories you could research one each and report back about your findings at an agreed time, but remember to read key sources for yourself and acknowledge them in your writing. Supporting each other will make the research process more efficient and enjoyable, so collaborate with colleagues to locate information for your projects.

Begin with what you know

The aim of the lectures and other teaching sessions on your course is to prepare you for producing the written assessments, so if you have attended these regularly you should have some relevant knowledge before you begin writing an assignment. Try to take full notes when you attend any kind of class and keep these safe as a starting point for your writing projects. Begin by re-reading your notes and the handouts you received before you start to write, and jot down important points or ideas sparked by reviewing this information. Your tutors will probably provide tips about useful sources, which will be good starting points for your research.

If you find yourself in a situation where your knowledge about a topic is limited or you were unable to attend all the relevant classes, you can take some useful steps to gather together information. First, look on your module web if this is relevant and download any advice that is available about the writing you have to do. Secondly, as soon as possible contact your module tutor to make an appointment to attend at an office hour or at another suitable time. Do some preparation for this meeting, such as reading your assignment brief and making a list of questions about issues you find confusing. You could also attempt to make a plan for your writing and take this along to seek advice, or draw up a shortlist of possible sources and ask whether you have missed anything important. Thirdly, contact a classmate and ask for some tips on understanding the assignment and locating relevant sources. You could offer to help in return by reading your classmate's draft and offering constructive feedback. Or you could offer to report back on sources you locate which could be mutually useful, but be clear that you do not wish to copy or allow your classmate to copy your work.

READILY AVAILABLE SOURCES

With a little effort you can expand the range of sources which are readily available to you by using your university library's catalogue to locate a diversity of online and paper-based resources (Hacker 2006: 9).

Literature searches

Using the tips below and keeping in mind the need to be systematic, learn how to search for the literature you need for your writing. You should consult a range of different types of sources, including books, journal articles, magazines, reference works, and audiovisual sources. Although much of the source material you need is available digitally, it can be helpful to locate paper-based sources, and do not neglect the older materials and seminal works in your field because they can give you a useful grounding in your subject area.

Library catalogue

Library catalogues are gateways to a wealth of sources produced for academic audiences, and without exploiting this access to scholarly materials you cannot fulfil the central requirements of advanced level study to read widely and research independently. Although most library catalogues are intuitive to use you will benefit from attending training sessions, or reading the self-help guides available in your library and usually also downloadable from the library website.

Databases

Databases are repositories of such extensive information that they can be daunting at first, but the time you invest in learning how to use them may yield the best returns of any skill you master at university. Students who avoid databases do themselves an injustice because they shut the door on the richest selection of relevant, reliable, and readily available materials there is (Hacker 2006: 9).

Training in how to navigate around databases and use them efficiently is available at every university library, either as part of an induction programme or on request. The advantage of seeking individual training from a library specialist is that you can ask about the databases most relevant for your discipline or research project. If possible, make an appointment with a subject specialist who will give you inside information on the best places to start your search for information. As you spend time learning how to use databases you will develop your own expertise about their usefulness for different types of writing. Some databases provide access to a broad range of articles and books and these can be helpful as you begin to search, while others focus on discipline-based topics and are invaluable when you narrow down a topic for your writing.

Make sure you are equipped to work online at home by checking at your library to find out if you need a password to access databases off-campus. Whether or not you require a password to authenticate your access, you will benefit from advice about the best way to locate digital sources remotely because the route may differ from the approach you use on university computers.

Searches in catalogues and databases

Ask library specialists to advise you about the protocol for searching for sources within the databases which are most relevant for your studies (Lunsford 2008: 235). Here are some general tips, but be aware that usage can vary, so you also need to familiarise yourself with the relevant system for you:

- Attend the training sessions on using databases, search engines, and catalogues at your library
- Seek individual advice from library specialists and see the guidance on the library website
- Make notes about how to search because databases vary and it is easy to forget the individual systems
- Decide on a broad search topic to start with
- Narrow your search as soon as you can
- Be ready to discard general sources in favour of more relevant materials
- Keep notes or use a reference management system.

Although public access search engines (like Google™) are easy to use and may yield interesting general results, relying on these exclusively does not constitute scholarly practice and will severely limit the type of sources you can access. Experiment with the search engines available via your university library website and you will substantially enrich your options and access to scholarly sources (Hacker 2006: 11, Lunsford 2009: 159).

When searching:

- Decide whether to search for a key word, subject, or author depending on the options available in a database, search engine, or catalogue
- Input a key word or words for your broad search topic
- Use the advanced options to narrow your search
- Use 'and' to extend your search
- Use 'or' to distinguish between key words
- Use 'not' to refine your search
- Use double quotation marks to narrow your search like this: "academic and writing"
- Use brackets to target your search like this: (academic writing)
- Use a star to search for variations of a key word (such as write and writing) like this: write*.

Reference management systems

You can make a paper-based or a digital list of the sources you locate which appear to be appropriate for your writing. Alternatively, you can benefit from tools to help you with this time-consuming task such as RefWorks™ and EndNote™. These reference management systems are usually available via university libraries, which often provide training and support. If you are unfamiliar with these tools you should enquire at your library or ask your tutors, because once you have learnt how to use them reference management systems can save you vast amounts of time.

Special collections

Find out whether your university library has an audiovisual collection or any other specialist holdings and visit these sections to meet the specialists and familiarise yourself with the materials. You can enhance your research or writing by drawing on archives, media, or artwork which may give you a fresh angle on your topic and enable you to undertake innovative work (Lunsford 2009: 163).

Interlibrary loan and document supply

If you find out about a source that is not held in your university library and you have started to search early enough, you can take advantage of the interlibrary loan system which enables you to order material from other collections (Lunsford 2009: 163). Often you are required to complete a form that has been signed by your tutor, so find out about the protocol at your university library and plan ahead with your search for sources. Gaining access to relevant sources your library does not hold can give you an edge as a researcher and boost the quality of your work.

RELIABLE SOURCES

What constitutes reliability may vary depending on your task, but in essence you need to find the right tools for the job each time you undertake a piece of writing (Hacker 2006: 6). You also need to be assured that the content of your sources is accurate, wellfounded, and well expressed, because this will help you draw on the contents for your own work.

Digital media

Select internet sites and other digital media with care because the material may be inaccurate, incomplete, or inappropriate for academic writing (Hacker 2006: 31). Be cautious if you think the material was designed to manipulate readers or favour a particular stance. In certain cases it is useful to discuss this bias in your academic writing, but, while internet sites provide general information to get people thinking about a topic, they are not always relevant as sources for scholarly writing. You can take a number of precautions to improve the likelihood of locating useful sources online by considering the following three points.

Who is the author?

In addition to the corporate author of the website it is often possible to identify the name of a contributor or the person who wrote particular articles. This is a good sign because authors who research their material and take care to present it clearly are most likely to put their name to their work. If you can identify an author you could try using a search engine such as Google™ to check this person's affiliation, such as a university, research group, or professional organisation. This is not always important, but it is a good approach to consider who produced digital material and what the main aim might be (Hacker 2006: 25, Lunsford 2009: 171).

Are the contents attributed or acknowledged?

One sign that a website is valuable for your own writing is clear and consistent acknowledgement of sources. Although it is not always appropriate, most topics demand research and you should avoid using sites which fail to credit the material that is borrowed from elsewhere. If the authors of websites have not acknowledged their sources, you could cite material in the usual way, giving full acknowledgement to the site you have consulted, but still be accused of copying.

This is because a plagiarism detection service such as Turnitin™ can identify the unacknowledged source and may interpret the fact that you have not cited it as an intentional omission of credit. Do not think that you can solve this problem by failing to cite the website you have read because this will also be identified. So, while it can be useful to read websites before you get into more targeted research for a project, you should only borrow material from sites which follow the same scholarly codes of practice you are expected to uphold at university, because otherwise your sources could seriously let you down.

Who is the intended audience?

As you read any website you should assess the intended audience, which might be professionals in a certain field, researchers in a subject area, or scholars. Only borrow material from sites intended for scholarly use unless they happen to be relevant for your project, for example because they contain specialist information or they form part of your research topic (Lunsford 2009: 164).

Always distinguish the informal style used for writing on the internet from the academic language you are required to produce at university. Never emulate the phrasing used on websites, because even brilliant ideas will be obscured by poor written expression. This means that if you borrow ideas from internet sites it may be best to paraphrase or summarise material, so in effect you are translating material from a colloquial style into academic English.

GENERAL SOURCES

Start your research process by locating sources which provide general information about your topic. These may include:

- Dictionaries
- Encyclopaedias
- Textbooks
- Internet sites
- Newspapers
- Magazines.

The kinds of general sources you need depend upon the purpose and audience of your particular project, but every written assessment requires an initial stage of consolidating your knowledge about the topic in general (Lunsford 2009: 156). Consider which of these sources are appropriate for each piece of writing you undertake.

Dictionaries

Although the value of dictionaries is often overlooked in the initial stages of research, you might find it useful to look up key terms used in your assignment brief so that you are clear from the outset about what you are being asked to do. Your assignment brief may contain important instructions that you need to carry out in order to succeed. For example, you may be asked to **discuss** a topic, **analyse** data, or **evaluate** information. These key terms have distinctive meanings, and they imply different kinds of writing in different disciplinary contexts, so you should check with your tutor that you understand their application in your own field.

Encyclopaedias

Many people read encyclopaedias for general interest but omit to consult them for academic writing. They are useful to provide quick access to facts and fill in the basic context to boost your understanding of a general topic. Usually encyclopaedias are accessed online, but use your own judgement to assess the quality of online resources before you borrow material for your academic writing (Hacker 2006: 14).

For instance, the online source Wikipedia is used by many writers to get started on a topic, but if you choose to consult this source remember that anyone can contribute an article and consequently there is a danger that the information is inaccurate. To prevent yourself repeating errors you can check an alternative source, preferably a more scholarly one such as a textbook. If the information is corroborated you can use it for your writing, but it is often preferable to borrow information from the more scholarly source and cite that in accordance with your chosen referencing style.

Some tutors will not consider digital sources such as Wikipedia to be appropriate types of information for advanced level study owing to the lack of quality control. You can ask your tutor about this issue, but avoid using inappropriate sources you have accessed online or elsewhere because they can undermine the quality of your writing. On the other hand, the list of references accompanying the articles in Wikipedia can be very helpful in providing suggestions for general sources to consult.

Textbooks

Textbooks are particularly useful for gathering general information about a subject, and books recommended by your tutors are the best place to start. Use the contents page and the index to decide where to focus your reading so you do not waste time covering material that is not relevant for a particular assignment. Also consult the references and recommended reading lists for more targeted information on particular topics. Although textbooks provide information in an efficient way, they are designed to offer only an introduction, so you should read more advanced sources when you have become familiar with your topic in general.

Newspapers

Reading broadsheets like the *Guardian, The Times*, and the *Independent* is an excellent way to gather general information on current affairs, political debates, and economic issues, and in the course of regular reading you might come across articles about the subjects you are studying at university. Owing to the brevity of newspaper articles they are most likely to provide introductory ideas or give you a new angle on your topic, which can be a useful starting point. However, it is essential to progress to more in-depth information for your writing. You should also be aware that, except for certain assignments, tutors may not consider newspapers appropriate sources and will instead expect you to begin reading recommended readings and then conduct independent research to locate more specific information. Importantly, you should not emulate the journalistic style of newspapers, which is too informal for academic writing.

Magazines

Reading magazines like the *National Geographic* is another good way to gain awareness about general interest topics, and you may find an article dedicated to an issue you are writing about. The journalistic form and style of magazines is not usually appropriate for written assessments at university, so consider your own use of language carefully and try to locate additional, more scholarly, sources to inform your thinking and writing.

SPECIFIC SOURCES

When you have identified some general sources, the next step is to locate specific sources that will provide further insights into the subject about which you are writing. Most written assessments are set to help you gain knowledge and understanding which you can apply in new contexts; for instance, in your future career. So, you should use the process of researching and writing to demonstrate your ability to manage, synthesise, and communicate information. Specific sources may include:

- Journal articles
- Chapters in edited collections
- Chapters in monographs
- Dissertations
- Theses
- Reports.

Journal articles

There are five main reasons for locating scholarly journal articles as sources for your projects:

1 Journal articles focus on a specific topic and they engage with scholarship in that area

2 Journal articles are relatively short, so they offer a quick way to becoming familiar with a subject or debate

3 Journals are often available digitally, so you can access them easily via the databases provided on your university library website

4 Journals are usually produced four times per year, so articles allow you to access the most up-to-date research in your field

5 Journal articles are produced according to the style and format commonly used in academic disciplines, which means that not only the content but also the form is a valuable model for your own academic writing.

Although journal articles may appear to be a bit formal and technical to start with, the more you read the easier they become to understand. It is not usually necessary to read through an entire volume of a journal; instead use a database to select the articles which relate to the topic about which you are writing.

Time spent familiarising yourself with scholarly journal articles is very well invested because they provide excellent exemplars for your own writing. It is often useful to emulate the syntax, terminology, and phrasing of articles from your academic discipline to improve your written expression. Obviously you must cite any material you borrow for your writing, but it is acceptable to keep a notebook and jot down signal phrases, verbs, and terms used by scholarly authors to enhance your own vocabulary. For example, if you are simply re-using transition phrases or terms to integrate research into an argument and you are not borrowing other people's **ideas** then it may not be necessary to cite and reference. If you are unsure, you should acknowledge your source, and remember that the golden rule is that you need to credit the intellectual property of others.

Chapters in edited collections

Although you may not have time to read entire books as you move into researching specifically relevant sources, you should try to locate chapters on your topic. Often edited collections bring together specialists in a particular field, or explore themes relevant to your work. The relatively short length of chapters gives you an easy way into complex subjects, and as chapters in edited collections are self-contained they can offer a stand-alone synopsis or an interesting angle on relevant subjects. Also, the style in which chapters in edited collections are written is usually a good example of academic prose which you might want to emulate in your own writing.

Chapters in monographs

Monographs are whole books usually written by a single author based on research projects or doctoral theses. They are invaluable for providing extensive information on a specific topic and are well worth locating, not only for the content but also for the scholarly style in which they are written and the specialist language employed. However, owing to the constraints of time it is often wise to target particular chapters or to consult the index to find the most relevant passages.

Dissertations

Dissertation is the term used in the UK for research projects produced in the final year of undergraduate study or for the postgraduate degree Master of Arts, Master of Science, MPhil, and other higher qualifications. These degrees take 1 or 2 years to complete and the dissertation explores a research question in some depth.

Dissertations are usually accessible via your university library, and as they are targeted at a specific research question they can be extremely useful as a specific source for your writing. The references may be especially valuable in providing leads for your research, and as the conventions for writing dissertations vary in each subject area, may offer a model for your own work. The quality of dissertations can be variable, so you should use this resource with a particularly critical eye.

Theses

Thesis is the term used in the UK for the extended research project submitted for a PhD, DPhil, or doctorate. The length is usually equivalent to a book, and theses are sometimes revised for publication as monographs to disseminate the research in the public sphere. Many theses are not formally published but, like dissertations, they are accessible via your university library. If you identify an especially interesting thesis, it is also possible to purchase a hard copy via the British Library. You should target individual chapters or sections that are most relevant for your research by consulting the list of contents, and you should examine the references to check for sources which may prove useful for your own writing.

Reports

Reports produced by corporations, industries, organisations, government depart-ments, research groups, and other official bodies can provide invaluable data for your own writing. Reports are often accessible online and can provide unique insights into the issues you are researching. Always apply the criteria outlined in the next section to assess the purpose and intended audience of reports so you can read them with a critical eye. Reports are usually written from a particular viewpoint, so there may be an inherent bias in the presentation of data, findings, and conclu-sions drawn. Like other public documents, reports are usually written with an agenda, but as long as you can identify a report's main aim and you critique the methodology you will find this kind of specific source helpful in boosting the quality of your work (Lunsford 2009: 172). The style of report writing in professional spheres may be the same as the conventions you are required to adhere to at university, but you might be required to structure your report in an alternative way and use more academic language, so check with your tutor before emulating the organisation and style of reports, especially those you access online.

SUMMARY

This chapter has stressed the value of systematic searching for sources by considering the relevance, ready availability, and reliability of materials. This focused approach to research will help you avoid wasting time because, with these criteria in mind, you are less likely to consult literature that is inappropriate or inadequate for your task.

The main arguments in this chapter:

- Get training and advice on how to use the catalogue and databases provided by your university library
- Get the right tools for the job each time you start a piece of writing by locating relevant sources
- Be prepared to reject irrelevant material at an early stage.

QUIZ

1 Why is it essential to learn how to search for sources via your university library catalogue?

2 To develop a systematic approach to searching for sources, which three Rs should you remember?

3 What is the main benefit of consulting sources which have been peer-reviewed?

4 Should you start by searching for specific or general sources first?

5 What is a monograph?

AVOIDING PLAGIARISM

This chapter suggests ways of maintaining academic integrity, including the KnACK strategy for avoiding plagiarism. This strategy entails **Kn**owing what you are doing, **A**cknowledging your sources, **C**reating your own perspectives, and being prepared to **K**eep revising your position to strengthen the originality of your work. This chapter highlights the importance of effective time management and suggests why some students plagiarise so you can avoid common pitfalls and improve your own chances of academic success.

The chapter covers:

- Defining plagiarism
- Avoiding plagiarism
- Time management
- A positive approach to citing and referencing
- Penalties for plagiarism.

Using this chapter

From Chapter 2 of *Academic Research, Writing & Referencing*, 1/e. Mary deane.

INTRODUCTION

Having introduced the concept of academic integrity, this chapter defines plagiarism and provides tips on avoiding unintentional plagiarism.

WHAT IS PLAGIARISM?

Plagiarism is the omission of acknowledgements when you borrow ideas, images, statistics, or other data from sources, or the attempt to present the intellectual property of another person as your own (Neville 2007: 28). Marsh (2004) offers the following comment about definitions of plagiarism as a negative act:

> Most generic plagiarism definitions – drawing on the Latin *plagium* ('net to entangle game') – stress that plagiarism is stealing, kidnapping, or theft of intellectual property.
>
> (Marsh 2004: 428)

Although plagiarism is penalised at university, learning how to avoid it also represents a chance to learn ways of improving your research and writing so, rather than focusing on problems you might encounter, try concentrating on the opportunity to learn new strategies for generating and disseminating knowledge in a scholarly fashion (Howard 2007: 13).

A positive approach

Many writers worry about plagiarism and find that this stress has a negative impact on their experience of university or their academic performance. While it is important to adopt the codes of academic practice outlined in the introduction, the more you enjoy discovering information and generating your own ideas, the less likely you are to plagiarise unintentionally.

Although you may not be aware of it, you make decisions about whether or not to plagiarise all the time; for instance, by reading this book you are choosing to learn about scholarly practice to prevent plagiarism in your work. So, you can relax to some extent because you are raising your game academically by seeking this guidance. Build upon this excellent start by thinking about your written assessments for yourself and acknowledging all the ideas, information, images, statistics, and other data from which you borrow for your own writing.

DEVELOPING A KnACK FOR AVOIDING PLAGIARISM

Learning how to avoid plagiarism takes patience and perseverance, especially if this approach to research and writing is new to you. The opposite of plagiarising is generating new knowledge, and the tips below help you to make this your priority. The simple way to avoid plagiarism is to produce your own work and credit the work of others using an appropriate system for citing and referencing sources. More specifically, you can avoid accidental plagiarism by focusing on what you know or think about the subject you are discussing in your writing.

Here are four tips to help you get the KnACK for generating ideas of your own:

1 **Kn**ow what you are doing for each written assessment
2 **A**cknowledge your sources
3 **C**reate your own perspective based upon research
4 **K**eep revising your position to strengthen the originality of your work.

Often, the difference between a writer who plagiarises accidentally and one who does not, is the evidence of the latter's thought processes, which reveal to readers that the work is original. Following the KnACK approach to generating ideas will help you deepen your knowledge so you can make this learning apparent in your writing and receive the credit you are due when examiners give you feedback (Neville 2007: 12).

Know what you are doing for each written assessment

Unless you understand the task you have been set or the steps involved in completing your research project, it is impossible to carry it out successfully. Knowing what you need to do is therefore the first step to success and this is where you need to start generating ideas. Read any guidance you have been given and take time to brainstorm about the various ways you could tackle your task. Seek further advice if necessary, and, if appropriate, you could put together an initial plan and ask your tutor for comments.

Acknowledge your sources

At an advanced level it is unusual to receive a written assessment or to undertake work that does not draw on existing research, ideas, images, data, or information. Although it is not possible to generalise, tutors usually expect to see evidence of your research and acknowledgements within your writing each time you borrow material.

Create your own perspective based upon research

The advantage of taking this scholarly approach is that it enables you to isolate the intellectual property of others from your own thinking. As readers and examiners are mostly interested in your assessment of the subject, developing a knack for building on what others have argued is one route to academic success. So, whenever it is appropriate, try to use your acknowledgement of sources as a stepping stone to positing your own ideas.

Keep revising your position to strengthen the originality of your work

The generation of new perspectives and insights takes time, and unless you allow yourself the opportunity to refine your thinking you can undermine your chances of success. Talking about and jotting down your ideas are essential to finding ways of articulating them clearly and organising them for the highest impact upon readers. Therefore, revising your position about a subject is an important part of generating new ideas and this may allow you to make a contribution to knowledge in your field.

TIME MANAGEMENT

Effective time management is essential to avoiding plagiarism (DeVoss and Rosati 2002: 194). Do not make the mistake of ignoring your project if it is unclear from the start, and do not expect your tutors to respond to last minute queries. You can take advantage of your tutor's office hours or ask questions during classes if you need clarification about the purpose of your task, but remember that academics are extremely busy and may not receive your message in time to respond before the deadline. Moreover, advanced level study requires you to take responsibility for your own study and to plan ahead, so be aware that if you delay in getting started with your work it is not your tutor's role to accommodate this lack of organisation.

On the other hand, there are structures in place at every institution to support students who require advice about study skills, welfare, and any issues that affect their chances of academic success. Find out about the systems in place at your own university by enquiring at the library, the Students' Union, or other units such as the Disabilities Office, the Welfare Office, and the Academic Office. If you take steps to help yourself you will be well supported, but it is up to you to seek the advice you need to work effectively.

Tutors expect you to locate the sources they recommend on reading lists and in other documents, so you need to plan ahead to access books and journals at the earliest opportunity. This is especially true if colleagues may be seeking the same texts as you, and if you leave your research to the last minute you could be disadvantaged from the outset by a lack of relevant material.

However, if you do find yourself in this situation, try finding an electronic version of the books you need to read. Although search engines (such as Google™, for instance) can be problematic because they provide access to inaccurate, misleading, and unscholarly material, they also give you access to scholarly sources. Search for books you have been recommended via an online forum (for example, Amazon) and you can probably read useful extracts for your writing. Remember to record all the information you need to acknowledge the source in your chosen referencing style, including the page numbers. Record e-books in the appropriate format with the website address and the date you accessed the source.

Penalties for plagiarism

The two main categories of plagiarism are intentional and unintentional, and there are serious penalties for both kinds. A distinction is not necessarily made between these two categories because students are responsible for adopting scholarly practice and are expected to produce their own work to gain qualifications.

The penalties for plagiarism are set by individual institutions and these are usually outlined in the appropriate place on the university website and in the documentation distributed to students when they start a course. If you are unfamiliar with the penalties at your institution it is up to you to find out what they are, because they apply to you whether or not you know them in detail.

Depending on the extent and nature of a case of plagiarism, the penalties might include a mark of zero for an assignment, the outcome of fail for a course, or exclusion from the university. There are procedures in place at every university to give students who are suspected of plagiarism a fair hearing, and you can usually find this information listed under 'academic integrity', 'academic conduct', 'plagiarism', or related terms on your institution's website.

The main forms of plagiarism are shown in the box below (Neville 2007: 28).

Forms of plagiarism

Intentional plagiarism

- Omitting in-text citations in your writing
- Omitting sources in your list of references
- Omitting the list of references
- Taking material written by another person and submitting it as your own work
- Collusion, or co-writing an assignment with another person and submitting it as your own work
- Cheating in exams
- Purchasing an assignment on the internet and submitting it as your own work
- Attempting to gain credit for the same work twice by re-submitting all or part of a written assessment.

Unintentional plagiarism

- Inaccurate or incomplete in-text citations
- Inaccurate or incomplete list of references
- Poor quoting
- Poor paraphrasing
- Poor summarising.

Why study?

What is your main purpose for undertaking a degree? Is it to enhance your intellectual development generally, to learn about a new field specifically, to improve your chances of success professionally, or to enjoy the university environment? If you plagiarise either on purpose or by accident you are likely to undermine your purpose for studying, and you could also mar your academic record for the future. Howard (2007) asserts the importance of learning and points out that plagiarism undermines this activity:

> [P]lagiarism in the academy matters so dearly because writing assignments are intended to help students learn course materials and gain communication and thinking skills. If those assignments are undermined through plagiarism, none of that learning takes place, and the academic enterprise is itself endangered.
>
> (Howard 2007: 11)

The requirement to document sources explicitly and accurately is usually a feature of assessment criteria because tutors expect to see evidence of independent research. When critical thinking is a required part of an assessment, critiquing clearly documented sources is also valued. So, remember to incorporate acknowledged sources into your writing because this is the foundation upon which academic work is built.

WHY DO SOME WRITERS PLAGIARISE?

Reasons for unintentional plagiarism

There are many reasons why writers plagiarise by accident; for instance, they may lack confidence when it comes to documenting sources fully, or they may be unfamiliar with the conventions of research writing in their field (Neville 2007: 30).

Incomplete records

A common reason why writers plagiarise unintentionally is that they forget to record all the details necessary to cite and reference properly. It is much easier to keep notes as you go along than to hunt for sources at the last minute, so be organised and keep a record of the details you will need (Williams and Carroll 2009: 22).

Learn how to cite and reference the main types of sources you use and keep a manual or guide handy for the less common types of sources. Remember that documenting sources in your academic writing requires you to use your common sense when you encounter a source that you do not know how to reference. In this situation ask yourself whether it could be a variant on the format for a book, journal article, or website, and reference it in a clear and consistent manner.

Lacking confidence

Some writers plagiarise unintentionally because they are not sure how to cite and reference properly. If you are not clear about what to do, you are more likely to make unintentional errors, and the way to avoid this is to dedicate time to practising, and to take every opportunity to gain feedback from your tutors. You can also avoid accidental plagiarism by working with a friend and swapping texts to help each other spot omissions and errors. Often we cannot see our own mistakes, but we can easily identify problems in other people's work, so it can be invaluable to find a colleague and help each other out. Remember that collusion, or co-writing a piece of work that you submit as your own, is a form of plagiarism so only include your own ideas in your written assessments and credit the intellectual property you borrow from sources.

A different approach

Writers who travel to an English-speaking nation for their higher education may encounter a different approach to research and writing than that to which they are accustomed (Lunsford 2008: 284). Remember that acknowledging sources allows writers to build upon research to articulate their own ideas, which is valued very highly at English-speaking higher education institutions. If you need some tips, read the instructions you receive from your tutors and take advantage of training courses offered by the library, for instance, and if you have specific questions you should ask your tutor.

Similarly, writers who have recently started a higher education degree may find the conventions different from their previous experience. Not all schools and colleges require students to use referencing systems, and it can be very confusing at first. The best way to become more familiar with the conventions you should adopt at university is to read journal articles in your field. The added advantage is that journal articles show you how to present a scholarly argument based on evidence. Scholarly articles are superb examples of how to organise the shape and contents of advanced level writing, and in addition you will learn about your topic as you read.

Reasons for intentional plagiarism

There are also many reasons why writers plagiarise on purpose; for example, they may have poor time management skills or they might lack commitment to a course.

Time

Writers who are under the pressure of time sometimes choose to cheat by copying material without crediting the sources. There is no excuse for this, especially as the situation can be avoided by planning ahead. Although some people think that no one will notice, academics are expert at tracing the line of argument and analysing the style of texts so it is very easy for them to spot irregularities, differences in tone, and material taken from elsewhere. Plagiarism detection services such as Turnitin™ can identify use of unacknowledged material by scanning the contents and checking this against a comprehensive database of sources and academic assignments. For an informative critique of such services, see Marsh (2004).

Lacking commitment

Some writers do not appreciate the need to engage with the culture of scholarly writing and attributing ideas to authors. However, these are essential abilities to cultivate, and without learning how to research and reference effectively writers are un-likely to pass their courses. Some students do not realise that, in addition to the formal penalties for plagiarism, other consequences stem from not acknowledging sources:

- It obscures your efforts to search for relevant sources
- It hides the time you spend selecting sources
- It undermines your efforts to read and understand sources.

AVOIDING UNINTENTIONAL PLAGIARISM

You can avoid plagiarising unintentionally by displaying academic integrity as you research, write, and reference written assessments, reports, studies, and other kinds of academic work. Here are some tips to help you adopt a scholarly approach throughout your studies:

Tips on avoiding plagiarism

Research

- Do not forget to take full notes recording the details necessary to document your sources properly
- Jot down the page numbers for passages you may quote, paraphrase, or summarise
- Also note the page numbers for images, statistics, or other data you might borrow.

Writing

- Always introduce the ideas, images, data, and words you have borrowed from sources
- When appropriate, comment on the sources you integrate into your own writing
- Give page numbers as appropriate (when you refer to a specific page)
- Check your paraphrasing of passages is accurate
- Check your summarising of passages is accurate.

Referencing

- Learn how to use a reference management system such as EndNote or RefWorks
- Cite sources as you are writing in accordance with the recommended referencing style
- Give full details for each source you have cited in the list of references at the end of your work in accordance with the recommended referencing style
- Ask a friend to check your in-text citations and list of references.

WHAT DOES *NOT* REQUIRE REFERENCING?

There is an element of judgement involved in deciding when you need to acknowl-edge sources in your academic writing and when you do not (Neville 2007: 20). If you are unsure it is preferable to include an in-text citation rather than omit one in case you accidentally plagiarise a source. The conventions are distinct within disciplinary contents and, to help you learn about the practice in your field, you should read the texts your tutors have recommended. Notice in particular how authors do not docu-ment common knowledge or generally accepted facts (Lunsford 2009: 190). Here is a list of the types of material you do not usually need to cite and reference:

- **Your own ideas**
- **Your own work**
- **General knowledge.**

Your own ideas

You do not usually need to document your own ideas because they are your intellec-tual property. However, if you are unsure you should check this with your tutor because there may be exceptions. For instance, if you refer to work you have pub-lished or submitted for assessment already, it could be important for examiners to know this because an attempt to gain credit for the same piece of work twice is viewed as plagiarism.

Your own work

If you undertake research involving experimentation, data collection, or the genera-tion of results you do not usually need to document your findings, providing the material is your own intellectual property. If you report the views or ideas of others, for instance through interviews or focus groups, you should acknowledge their contributions although this can be done anonymously. Follow the guidelines for ethical research practices at your institution and seek specific advice from tutors or expert researchers in your field.

General knowledge

If you refer to common knowledge, such as the dates of world wars, well known myths, or well established facts, you do not usually need to document the source because general knowledge implies a general holding of the intellectual property. On the other hand, if you refer to an author or artist's interpretation of a story or event, this is the intellectual property of another person and it must be acknowl-edged with accurate citation and referencing.

SUMMARY

This chapter has suggested ways of maintaining academic integrity, including the KnACK strategy for avoiding plagiarism which entails **Kn**owing what you are doing, **A**cknowledging your sources, **C**reating your own perspective, and being prepared to **K**eep revising your position to strengthen the originality of your work. The chapter has highlighted the importance of effective time management and outlined potential reasons for plagiarising so you can avoid these pitfalls and improve your own chances of academic success.

The main arguments in this chapter:

■ You can take a positive and practical approach to avoiding plagiarism

■ This takes time and forward planning

■ It requires you to learn how to cite and reference

■ It also takes practice.

QUIZ

1 Here is an extract from an article by Lawson et al. (2009) called 'Does the Multi-lateral Matter?' Is this passage missing any in-text citations?

Does the Multilateral Matter?

The International Monetary Fund (IMF), the World Bank and the World Trade Organization (WTO) have a common origin in the conference held in Bretton Woods, New Hampshire during July 1944 and share a focus on multilateral cooperation. But each addresses a different aspect of international economic interaction. The IMF and World Bank were created to address international monetary cooperation and development issues respectively.

(Lawson et al. 2009: 2)

---

2 Read the examples below and decide whether the writers were correct to document this information.

Example 1

As part of her study, the author took the photograph in Figure 1 to illustrate the behaviour of cats.

Figure 1: Cats' involvement in human activities
(Long 2010).

Example 2

An increased consumption of calories with no additional exercise results in weight gain (Edwards 2010).

Example 3

The story of Cinderella is a well known fairytale (Grimm and Grimm 1812) which has long been popular.

Example 4

Scholars have argued that leadership is a quality possessed by everyone, and external conditions determine whether or not individuals fulfil their potential (Potterson 2008, Zinger 2010).

THE HARVARD STYLE

This chapter demonstrates how to use the Harvard style and provides a wide range of examples. The chapter stresses the importance of clear and consistent acknowledgement of sources, and points out that you need to use your own judgement when you are acknowledging unusual sources.

The chapter covers:

- Variations of the Harvard style
- In-text citations
- The list of references
- Written sources
- Secondary sources
- Numerical sources
- Audiovisual sources
- Digital formats.

Using this chapter

From Chapter 10 of *Academic Research, Writing & Referencing,* 1/e. Mary deane.

INTRODUCTION

This chapter explains how to cite and reference using the Harvard style. However, before adopting any referencing system you must consult the guidance given to you by your tutors and follow their advice. Course handbooks and assignment briefs usually specify which style you should use, and if in doubt you should ask your tutors or seek advice at your university library.

VARIATIONS OF THE HARVARD STYLE

There is no single version of the Harvard style because there is no official publication providing instructions on how to use this referencing system. Instead, you will find many different websites and manuals which all give slightly different advice. The existence of different versions of the Harvard style can create confusion because each version recommends slightly different use of punctuation, and sometimes different ways of formatting the pieces of information required for list of reference entries. For example, you may be advised to insert a comma after the author's surname, or write 'p.' instead of a colon before giving page numbers.

Do not let the existence of different variations of the Harvard style confuse you, but choose a version in consultation with your tutors and stick with it. The main aim of referencing is to show readers **where you have borrowed material from sources**, and, as long as this information is *clear and consistently formatted* you will be successful as a scholar and researcher.

TWO ELEMENTS

Whichever version of the Harvard style you use, there are two elements you need to master (Williams and Carron 2009: 7). The two elements are:

1 *In-text citations* every time you borrow material from a source

2 A *list of references* at the end of your work.

Your academic writing must contain both in-text citations and a list of references. In-text citations are acknowledgements of the author, date, and when appropriate the page number each time you borrow from a source. You should place in-text citations within brackets and insert a colon before the page number like this:

> Academic writing involves 'careful citation and critical thinking' (McArthur 2010: 5).

It is a serious omission not to cite the sources you refer to in your writing, and this omission constitutes *plagiarism* because it is a failure to acknowledge authors' intellectual property.

There are various ways of integrating sources into your own writing. When you borrow numerical data or images you should introduce these clearly, and if appropriate label them as figures or tables. When borrowing words and ideas, you can quote, paraphrase, summarise, and critique sources (Neville 2007: 36). Whichever method you choose to integrate sources into your own writing, you must give *an in-text citation* to acknowledge the material you borrow.

As mentioned above, in addition to your in-text citations you must make a list recording more information for each source you have cited. The most challenging aspect of referencing is to **learn the formula** for formatting different types of sources such as books, journal articles, and websites, but with practice this becomes increasingly easy.

IN-TEXT CITATIONS

As previously mentioned, the term 'in-text citation' means an acknowledgement of your sources each time you borrow material for your writing. The Harvard style is easy to use because you simply cite the author's surname, the date, and when appropriate the page numbers in brackets. When you borrow images or statistics, and when you quote, paraphrase, or summarise a short passage, you should usually give the page number. Here is an example:

Give the author's surname and the date, then insert a colon and give the page number enclosed within brackets ➡️

(Jones 2010: 34)

Here is another example:

The role of academic writing in assessment at university Accuracy and agility as a writer are essential to obtain good grades at university (Smith 2010: 4). According to Shah (2009: 7) strong written communication is one of the determining factors in success at this advanced level.

This example shows that each time you borrow from a source you should give the author's surname and date, plus the **page number if you refer to a specific page**. You can either name the authors in your own sentence, or give their surnames within your in-text citations, and you can vary this depending on the emphasis you want to give.

73

How to cite

You need to gather three pieces of information when you are making notes to produce accurate in-text citations. Ask yourself:

1 Who is the *author*?

If there are multiple authors, write them all down in your notes. If the author is an organisation or group of people this is known as the **corporate author**.

2 In which *year* was the source published?

If the source is digital, when was it last updated?

3 Do you need to give *page numbers*?

You usually do if you quote, paraphrase, summarise an extract from a specific page, borrow data, or use images from printed sources. Ask your tutor if you are unsure.

CITING WRITTEN SOURCES

You should also take note of the ways authors cite material in journal articles because these often provide models for academic writing in your own discipline. In particular, notice how authors integrate quotes, paraphrases, summaries, and critiques of sources as they develop their own ideas.

Multiple authors

It can be disruptive for readers if you cite a source with many authors because this interrupts the flow of your own writing. To avoid this, the convention when one source has many authors is to give the first author's surname, then use the Latin term 'et al.' which is an abbreviation of et alii meaning 'and others'. Note that you must insert a full stop after 'et al.' because it is an abbreviated term. Here is an example:

> Gillett et al. argue that writing is a core capability at university (2009: 54).

Remember that although you are writing one author's surname you are actually referring to multiple authors, so your own sentence must agree grammatically. It is inaccurate to write 'Gillett et al. argues' because you are referring to authors in the plural, so your own verb must agree.

Variations of the Harvard style give different recommendations about when to use 'et al.' and how to format this term. A common approach is to use et al. when there are more than *two* authors. However, some variations of the Harvard style recommend using et al. when there are more than three authors. Similarly, some variations of the Harvard style require you to italicise *et al.* thus because it is a Latin term and foreign phrases are often italicised in academic writing.

The examples below offer further advice on using in-text citations in the Harvard style.

Mentioning authors at the start of sentences

You can refer to an author directly and cite the source near the start of your sentence like this:

> McCutcheon (2010: 43) argues that academic writing cannot be taught generically, but must be explored as an 'integral part' of disciplinary studies.

Mentioning authors at the end of sentences

Alternatively, you can refer to an author directly and cite the source near the end of your sentence so it does not disrupt the flow of your argument, like this:

> McCutcheon argues that academic writing cannot be taught generically, but must be explored as an 'integral part' of disciplinary studies (2010: 43).

Giving authors within in-text citations

You can give the author's name in your in-text citation rather than in your own sentence like this:

> Academic writing cannot be taught generically, but must be explored as an 'integral part' of disciplinary studies (McCutcheon 2010: 43).

As you will see when you read scholarly journal articles, authors tend to use all three approaches in their writing. Notice the most common way of citing in your subject area and adopt this, but also feel free to vary these three techniques to suit your own written style.

Citing more than one source

Be careful if you refer to more than one source in a single sentence because you must ensure that your readers can identify which author has made which point. Look at the two examples of citing below. Which is clearer?

Example 1: many citations in a list

> Recent research into road safety recommends a revised approach to teaching children how to cross roads through national education programmes and local initiatives (Anderson 2000: 3, Potter 2001: 54, Scott 2003: 6, Jones and Sharma 2009: 87).

In the example above, the writer has cited four sources in one sentence so the reader is unclear what each source is about.

Example 2: many citations clearly distinguished

> Recent research into road safety recommends a revised approach to teaching children how to cross roads through national education programmes (Potter 2001: 54, Scott 2003: 6) and local initiatives (Anderson 2000: 3, Jones and Sharma 2009: 87).

In the second example the writer has listed only two sources in each in-text citation so that readers are much clearer which authors made which points. When you are citing sources try to make it clear who made which point and avoid listing many texts at once because this can confuse readers. If your in-text citations are precise they are more helpful for readers who are interested in your topic.

The order for listing citations

When you list a number of citations in one sentence you should think about the order. Check the guidelines in your chosen referencing style and be consistent. Notice that in the example above, the citations are given in chronological order with the oldest first. Some referencing styles recommend listing the most recent source first, so check with your tutor if you are unsure.

Page numbers and in-text citations

Every time you quote, paraphrase, or summarise a short section you should usually give the page number, unless you are using a digital source that does not contain page numbers.

The same applies when you borrow *images* or *numerical data*. Basically, whenever you borrow from a particular page your readers may need to know the page number to locate that page for themselves. However, check with your tutor as practice can vary in different disciplines.

There are three main reasons for giving page numbers. First, it demonstrates your professionalism and conveys your ability to make notes in a scholarly way. Secondly, it helps readers track down the passages, images, and data you have borrowed and consult this information themselves. Thirdly, examiners may want to check you have understood a source, and they will not be impressed if you do not leave a clear account of exactly where in your source you have referenced. In general, omitting page numbers gives an impression of laziness, so avoid this by jotting down the page numbers when you are making notes, and include them in your in-text citations whenever you quote, paraphrase or refer to a specific page.

Why give page numbers?

1. To show professionalism
2. To help readers track down the passages, images, and data you have borrowed
3. To meet marking criteria and show examiners you can cite in a scholarly fashion.

Page numbers and paraphrasing

Most versions of the Harvard style advise you to give page numbers when you paraphrase a passage from a source. This is because, although when you paraphrase you put an author's ideas into your own words, borrowing material in this way is not very different from quoting.

Page numbers and summarising

There are two different ways of summarising material; one of which is to summarise the whole source, and the other is to summarise a short section of a source. If you summarise an entire book or journal article you do not need to provide the page numbers in your in-text citations. However, if you summarise a specific passage you should give the page number in case readers wish to locate the passage. You will need to use your judgement when deciding whether or not to give page numbers, but it is better to give pages unnecessarily than to omit them when they are required. In particular, some examiners may penalise writers who quote without giving the page numbers.

CITING SECONDARY SOURCES

Secondary sources are sources cited in the texts you read. They are 'secondary' because you have not seen them yourself. If you can locate the original sources and cite them as usual this demonstrates your research skills. As secondary sources are sometimes reported inaccurately, locating them for yourself helps you avoid bringing errors into your work.

However, if you are unable to locate the original source, you must make it clear to readers that you are citing a source you have not seen. To cite a secondary source, give the author of the secondary source and the date, then write 'cited in' and give the author, date and page number of the source you have read. Here is an example of citing a secondary source:

> Academic writing demands time, planning, and commitment (Adams 2007 cited in Downs 2010: 34).

CITING NUMERICAL SOURCES

Give an in-text citation acknowledging the author or statistician each time you borrow statistics, graphs or other numerical data from sources. Follow the same basic practice for citing numerical data as you would for citing written sources. You will often have to make a judgement about who to cite as the author, and this will depend on the purpose of your writing. Here is an example of citing statistics:

> A recent survey indicates that 24% of pet owners rescued their animals from homes or charities (Pets Research 2010: 32).

When you borrow numerical data from a specific page in a printed source you should give the *page number* so readers can locate the same place in the source with ease.

Depending on the nature of your writing, it may be useful to put numerical data into a table. This is particularly appropriate if you are writing a substantial piece of work such as a report, dissertation or thesis. If you do this you should give the figure a title and produce a contents page for your document, including a list of figures. Remember to discuss the significance of the data (see Figure 10.1).

CITING AUDIOVISUAL SOURCES

Just as you integrate written sources into your writing using different techniques such as quoting, paraphrasing, summarising, and critiquing, you should also integrate audiovisual sources into your writing in a scholarly fashion. Figure 10.1 shows how to cite numerical data.

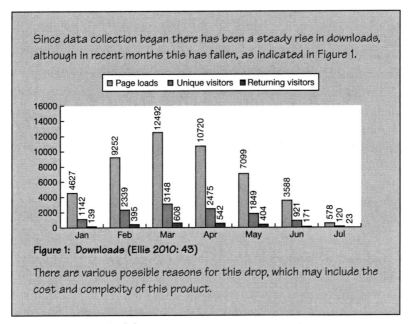

Since data collection began there has been a steady rise in downloads, although in recent months this has fallen, as indicated in Figure 1.

Figure 1: Downloads (Ellis 2010: 43)

There are various possible reasons for this drop, which may include the cost and complexity of this product.

Figure 10.1 **Numerical data**

Always assess the value of sources before borrowing from them for your work and be clear about the purpose they serve. Remember to give the page number when you borrow data and images from printed sources.

Introduce each audiovisual source as you introduce it into your writing and comment on it as appropriate. If you are writing a substantial document such as a report, dissertation, or thesis you should label the images as figures and include a list of figures in your list of contents. Figure 10.2 shows how to cite visual sources.

Citing films, videos, and DVDs (not downloaded)

For this type of source you need to decide who to cite as the author, and most commonly it is appropriate to cite the director or producer. Here is an example of citing a DVD:

In *Cold Mountain*, Kidman brings the American Civil War to life (Minghella 2004).

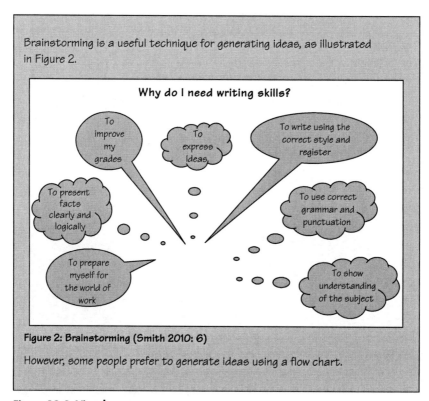

Figure 10.2 **Visual sources**

CITING DIGITAL FORMATS

Many different types of sources are available digitally, so the best way to support you in documenting your digital sources is to provide some general guidelines for you to adopt as appropriate for your different writing projects.

Quality control and online sources

Websites can be very useful as leads for future research; for example, the website Wikipedia is not subject to scholarly review so anyone could make an inaccurate contribution and it would be unfortunate to repeat errors in your own work. On the other hand, the references supplied within Wikipedia articles are potentially valuable if you follow them up and assess their value for your own use.

It is vital to analyse the quality of online sources before you draw on material for your academic writing (Hacker 2006: 31). Some online sources are unreliable or inaccurate and therefore inappropriate for use in academic writing. Be aware, for instance, that translations may not be accurate. The danger of citing unreliable sources is that this can undermine the quality of your own work, so before using online sources, consider whether it is worth consulting more scholarly sources instead.

Corporate authors

If a source is not written by people, but instead is produced by an organisation or professional body, this is known as a 'corporate author'. When citing from sources created by an organisation you should cite the corporate author.

It is not always easy to identify the author of a website, but as long as you give the same details in your in-text citations as in your list of references your readers will be able to locate the source for themselves. This is because your list of references entry will contain the full website address (URL) (see Figure 10.3).

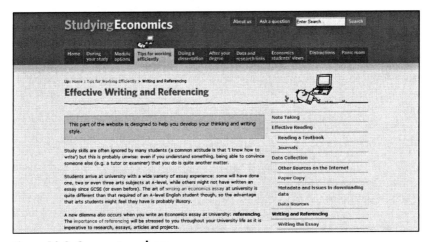

Figure 10.3 **Corporate authors**

To locate the author of online sources, check the bottom of a webpage to see if there is an acknowledgement or any copyright information. In Figure 10.3, although it is not visible, on this website it says at the bottom of the page:

> © The Economics Network of the Higher Education Academy, University of Bristol.
>
> Supported by the Royal Economic Society.

The corporate author here is the Economics Network because the copyright symbol © signals that the intellectual property rights belong to this group. To cite this corporate author you would write:

(Economics Network 2009)

Notice that you do *not* give the website address (URL) within in-text citations because it would disrupt the flow of your own writing. Instead the website address is recorded in your list of references.

Dates and online sources

It is often difficult to find a date within online sources. Check the information at the bottom of the webpage if you cannot see the date at first, and you might find the date when the site was last updated, which you can use for your in-text citations. If no date is given, you can either estimate and give the year you are viewing if recently updated, or write 'n.d.', meaning 'no date', like this:

> (Economics Network n.d.)

Page numbers and online sources

Online sources do not have page numbers, so it is usual practice to omit page numbers for in-text citations of online sources. This is acceptable because readers who wish to locate these sources can use the website address (URL) given in your list of references.

Downloads

Digital media are often available as podcasts and in other formats which allow you to listen to programmes again. To acknowledge these sources when you borrow material for your own writing, you should cite the author and date in brackets. You are the best person to decide which author to cite as you acknowledge your sources, and as long as you link the in-text citations to entries in your list of references your readers will be able to locate the sources for themselves. Below are some examples.

Citing the speaker as author

You can refer directly to the speaker as the author like this:

> As part of the BBC programme *In our time with Melvyn Bragg*, John Haldane discussed the life of St Thomas Aquinas (2009).

Citing the organisation as corporate author

Or, you can refer to the corporate author like this:

> As part of the programme *In our time with Melvyn Bragg*, John Haldane discussed the life of St Thomas Aquinas (BBC Radio 4 2009).

Citing personal communications

To cite a personal communication, quote, paraphrase, or summarise and give the author's surname and the date. Either mention the author in your own writing or in your in-text citation. Here is an example in which the author is mentioned directly:

> In a personal communication Professor Saunders explained his theory in depth (2009).

Citing blogs

To cite a blog, quote, paraphrase, or summarise and give the author's surname and the date. Either mention the author directly, or in your in-text citation. Here is an example in which the author is mentioned in the in-text citation:

> 'This week something great happened: two of my former students connected with me' (Dwyer 2009).

Citing online discussion fora and mailing lists

To cite an online discussion list or listserv, quote, paraphrase, or summarise and give the author's surname and the date. Here is an example in which the author is mentioned in the in-text citation:

> 'Interrogating our approach is essential' (Harris 2009).

Decisions about citing

This section of Chapter 10 has explained how to cite using the Harvard style. It has covered the main points you need to know and recommended that you seek advice from your tutors when you are unsure about any aspect of citing and referencing. It has stressed that there are times when you have to make **decisions** about how to cite sources in your writing. Base these decisions on the following three rules:

1 Be *clear* about where in your writing you have borrowed from sources

2 Be *consistent* as you make choices about which information to cite as the author and date

3 Be *comprehensive* in giving the author, date, and page numbers (when appropriate).

THE LIST OF REFERENCES

A list of references is a full record of all the sources you have cited in your writing. The purpose of this list is to provide all the details readers require to locate your sources for themselves. The example below demonstrates how to produce a list of references.

List of References

Abrahams, B. (2010) *Academic Writing in the United Kingdom*. London: Routledge

Carr, S. (2009) *Writing for success: Assessment in higher education*. Maidstone: HarperCollins

Potter, H. (2005) *An Introduction to Human Anatomy*. 4th edn. London: Adam Arnold available from <http://anatomy/introduction/human/htm> [27th March 2006]

There is a specific format for referencing each different type of source. For printed sources you should record the publication details, and for online sources you should provide the website address and the date you accessed the data.

THE LINK BETWEEN IN-TEXT CITATIONS AND THE LIST OF REFERENCES

As previously mentioned, every source that is given in your in-text citations must be fully recorded in your list of references.

The most efficient way to ensure that all the sources you cite are recorded in your list of references is to compile both elements as you are drafting your work. You should work hard to develop a method that works for you. Many scholars find reference management systems such as EndNote and RefWorks effective for this task (Neville 2007: 23, Williams and Carroll 2009: 78). Ask about these tools at your university library because they can save you lots of time.

How to construct a list of references

The list of references goes at the end of your document and the sources are listed in alphabetical order according to the authors. You should not subdivide this list into types of sources, but you do need to learn how to format the entries for different types of sources. The three main types of source you need to learn about are:

- **Books**
- **Journal articles**
- **Websites.**

Once you have mastered how to reference these three types of sources you will have enough knowledge to reference other source types because they are mostly variations of these three formats.

Use your judgement

Referencing requires you to exercise your **judgement**, especially when you need to document uncommon or unusual types of sources. When choosing a format, do not be afraid to adapt the formula for referencing a book, journal article, or website, depending on which is most appropriate for the source you want to cite and reference. The information below contains tips on referencing these three main types of sources and adapting the formats for less common types of sources.

REFERENCING BOOKS AND SIMILAR TYPES OF SOURCES

You usually require six pieces of information to reference a book. It can be difficult to find these six details but, with practice, you will become an expert. The tips below will help you to grow in confidence in finding and recording this information:

1 **Author**

2 **Date**

3 **Title**

4 **Edition, if relevant**

5 **Place of publication**

6 **Publisher.**

Books

Here is a book entry for the list of references with some explanation:

Give the author's surname and initial, then the date in brackets and the title in italics, followed by a full stop. Give the edition, if relevant, then the place of publication followed by a colon and the publisher

Jones, P. (2010) *Enhancing Academic Practice.* 2nd edn. Harlow: Pearson Education

E-books

If you are using an electronic book (e-book) or a digital format you need to add two more pieces of information. These are:

7 **The full website address (URL)**

8 **The date of access (when you viewed the source).**

The reason for giving the website address is so that readers can access the e-book for themselves. The reason for giving the date you accessed it online is that internet sites are regularly updated, so readers need to know when you viewed the book in case the interface has changed since then.

Here is an example of how to reference an e-book:

Give the author's surname and initial, then the date in brackets and the title in italics, followed by a full stop. Give the edition, if relevant, then the place of publication, followed by a colon and the publisher. Write 'available from' and give the full website address within chevrons (< >), followed by the date of access in square brackets ➡

> Potter, H. (2005) *An Introduction to Human Anatomy*. 4th edn. London: Adam Arnold available from <http://anatomy/introduction/human/htm> [27th March 2006]

Authors

On a book's cover (see below) you should find the name of the authors and the title. If there is more than one author you must record the names in the order you find them written on the book cover. This is because the order may signal the amount of work each author has done, with the person who produced the most material listed first. However, most often authors are listed alphabetically and you should reproduce this order as you document their work.

Figure 10.4 **Book authors and titles**

Editors

If a book has an editor instead of an author you should write (ed.) after the name and before the date like this:

Give the editor's surname and initial, then write 'ed.' in brackets, followed by the date in brackets. Give the title in italics followed by a full stop. Give the edition, if relevant, then the place of publication followed by a colon and the publisher

Long, H. (ed.) (2010) *Adventures in Sound*. 2nd edn. Oxford: Oxford University Press

If a book has both an editor and an author, you should give the author first and then the date followed by the editor like this:

Give the author's surname and initial, then the date in brackets. Write 'ed. by' and give the editor's surname and initial, then the title in italics followed by a full stop. Give the edition, if relevant, then the place of publication followed by a colon and the publisher

Smart, K. (2010) ed. by Knowles, G. *Scholarly Writing*. 2nd edn. Oxford: Oxford University Press

Translators

If the author is the translator you should give the author as usual, then acknowledge the translator after the title like this:

Give the author's surname and initial, then the date in brackets and the title in italics, followed by a full stop. Write 'Trans. by' then give the translator's surname and initial then the place of publication followed by a colon and the publisher

Hatter, P. (2010) *Social Welfare*. Trans. by Hatter, P. Oxford: Oxford University Press

If the translator is not the author as well you should give the author first then the translator.

Dates of publication

Dates can be confusing, but the most important year to record is usually the date a book was first published. This is given inside the cover with all the information about the printer and publishing house. In the example below, the year to cite and reference is 2006:

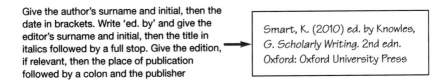

First published 2006

Reprinted 2007, 2008 (twice), 2010

Dates when a book was just **reprinted** are not relevant, so in the example above you would ignore the dates after 2006. Reprinted simply means that another set of copies was made and the contents of the book remain identical, so the convention is to continue to cite the date the book was first published.

Editions

However, if the book you are using is a new or revised *edition*, you should not record the first date given, but instead record the 2nd, 3rd, or revised edition date depending which one you read. A revised edition is usually indicated on the book's cover as well as inside in the initial pages, where you will usually find information like this:

> First published 2006
>
> Second edition published 2010

When a new edition of a book is produced, the author re-writes sections and often adds material to update the publication, so the page numbers change and readers need to know which edition you have read. In the example above you would cite and reference the date as 2010, the year the second edition was published. You must also indicate this fact in your list of references entry like this:

> Harrison, M. (2010) *Academic Writing: Tips and Tricks*. 2nd edn. Harlow: Pearson Education

Titles

If there is a subtitle you must include this detail in your list of references entry and add a colon before the subtitle like this:

> *Academic Writing: Tips and Tricks.*

Capitalisation when referencing books

Always consult the guidance your tutors provide on capitalisation when referencing books. Usually in the UK, significant words in book titles are capitalised, but check the instructions in your recommended referencing style.

Note that prepositions and conjunctions are not normally capitalised.

Place of publication

The place of publication is usually a city, and this information is given inside the book cover and usually also on the title page. If you see a list of several cities you should just record the first one, so London is the place to document from this list:

> London, New York, Paris, Milan.

You may come across the full address of the publisher like this:

> Edinburgh Gate
> Harlow
> Essex CM20 2JE
> England.

In this case you need to identify the city, which is Harlow in the example above. Essex is a county and England is a country, so you do not document these in your list of references.

Publisher

The publisher is relatively easy to identify because there is usually a logo or indication of who published a book on the front cover, and often on the spine of the book. The publisher is usually written inside the book cover in the initial pages, for example, like this:

> Pearson Education Limited.

In the example above you would not include the word 'Limited' but simply write 'Pearson Education' as the publisher.

So, if you put all five pieces of information together, your entry in the list of references for a book should be as shown in Table 10.1.

Table 10.1 **Books**

Author's surname and initial	Date	Book title	Edition	Place of publication	Publisher
Jones, B.	(2010)	Academic Writing: Tips and Tricks.	2nd edn.	Harlow:	Pearson Education

Other types of books

Edited collections

Edited collections are books containing chapters written by different authors. You will usually need to cite material from a specific chapter, so record the name of the chapter author, the chapter title, and the first and last page numbers for the chapter. In addition, document the same information you usually need to reference a book.

Here is an example of how to reference a chapter:

Give the surname and initial of the chapter author, then the date in brackets and the chapter title followed by a full stop. Write 'In', then the title of the edited collection in italics, followed by a full stop. Write 'Ed. by' then the editor's surname and initial followed by the place of publication followed by a colon and the publisher, then a colon and the page numbers of the article	Skillen, J. (2006) *Teaching Academic Writing from the 'Centre' in Australian Universities*. In *Teaching Academic Writing in UK Higher Education: Theories, Practices and Models*. Ed. by Ganobcsik-Williams, L. Houndmills: Palgrave Macmillan: 140–53

A note about referencing chapters in edited collections

Some referencing styles instruct you to put single quote marks around chapter titles. Follow your recommended guidelines and if unsure, check with your tutor.

So, your entry in the list of references for a chapter from an edited collection should be as shown in Table 10.2.

Table 10.2 **Edited collections**

Author's surname and initial	Date	Chapter title	Write 'In' then the title of the edited collection	Edition	Write 'Ed. by' then the editor's surname and initial	Place	Publisher	Page numbers of chapter
Skillen, J.	(2006)	Teaching Academic Writing from the 'Centre' in Australian Universities.	In *Teaching Academic Writing in UK Higher Education: Theories, Practices and Models.*		Ed. by Ganobcsik-Williams, L.	Houndmills:	Palgrave Macmillan:	140–53

Reports

The formula for referencing reports is similar to the method for referencing books. Here is an example of how to reference a report:

Give the author or corporate author and the date in brackets, then the title in italics followed by the number of the report and a full stop. Give the place the report was produced, and a colon, then the organisation or publisher

→

Dietetics Committee (2009) Department of Health Report on Dietary Health no. 41. London: Stationery Office

Pamphlets

The formula for referencing pamphlets, leaflets, and brochures is similar to the method for referencing books. Here is an example of how to reference a pamphlet:

Give the author or corporate author and the date in brackets, then the title in italics, followed by a full stop. Give the place the pamphlet was produced, and a colon, then the organisation or publisher

→

National Health Service (2009) Catch it, Bin it, Kill it. Coventry: University Hospital

Unpublished booklets, manuals, guides, and handbooks

The formula for referencing any unpublished source is similar to the method for referencing books. Here is an example of how to reference an unpublished booklet:

Give the author and the date in brackets, then the title, followed by a full stop. Give the place the source was produced, and a colon, then the organisation

→

Dawson, E. (2010) Guide to Writing Reports. Coventry: Coventry University

REFERENCING SECONDARY SOURCES

Secondary sources are sources cited in materials you have read, but you have not seen them yourself. To reference a secondary source, give the publication details for the secondary source, followed by the publication details for the source that you have read.

Here is an example of how to reference a secondary source:

For the secondary source, give the author's surname and initial, then the date in brackets and the title in italics, followed by a full stop. Give the place of publication followed by a colon and the publisher then a full stop. Write 'Cited in' then do the same for the source you have read

→

Adams, K. (2007) Researching and Writing. Harlow: Pearson Education. Cited in Downs, E. (2010) Strategies for Success. Harlow: Pearson Education

REFERENCING JOURNAL ARTICLES AND SIMILAR TYPES OF SOURCES

Journal articles

You usually need seven pieces of information to reference a journal article. These are:

1 Author

2 Date

3 Article title

4 Journal title

5 Volume number

6 Part or issue number (if there is one)

7 Page numbers of the article.

Here is an example with more information about the formula for referencing a journal article:

Give the author's surname and initial, the date in brackets, and the title of the article followed by a full stop. Give the title of the journal in italics, the volume number, the part (or issue) number in brackets, then the page numbers of the article

→

Elston, C. (2009) Making Group-work Work: An Overview. *Journal of Learning Development in Higher Education* 1 (1): 1–7

A note about referencing articles in journals

Some referencing styles instruct you to put single quote marks around article titles. Follow your recommended guidelines and if unsure, check with your tutor.

Accessing journal articles online

If you download an online journal article and your version is exactly the same as the hard copy in the journal, including the page numbers, you should reference the article as if you were using the hard copy. However, if the page numbers in your version are not the same as the hard copy in the journal you need to add two pieces of information. These are:

■ **The full website address (URL)**

■ **The date of access.**

Here is an example of how to reference an article you have accessed online when the page numbers are different to the hard copy in the journal:

If you are supplying the URL, write 'available from' and give the full website address within chevrons (< >), followed by the date of access in square brackets ➤

> Elston, C. (2009) Making Group-work Work: An Overview. *Journal of Learning Development in Higher Education* 1 (1): 1–8 available from <http://www.aldinhe.ac.uk/ojs/index.php?journal=jldhe&page=article&op=view&path%5B%5D=36&path%5B%5D=17> [1st October 2009]

So, your entry in the list of references for a journal article you have accessed online should be as shown in Table 10.3:

Table 10.3 **Journal articles**

Author's surname and initial	Date	Article title	Journal title	Volume no.	Part or issue no.	Page numbers of article	Full website address (URL)	Date of access
Elston, C.	(2009)	Making Group-work Work: An Overview.	Journal of Learning Development in Higher Education	1	(1):	1–8	available from <http://www.aldinhe.ac.uk/ojs/index.php?journal=jldhe&page=article&op=view&path%5B%5D=36&path%5B%5D=17>	[1st October 2009]

Newspapers and magazines

The formula for referencing articles in newspapers and magazines is similar to the method for referencing journal articles, and if you access a newspaper online you should include the website address in the same way. Here is an example of how to reference a newspaper article you have accessed online:

Give the surname and initials of the authors, the date in brackets, and the title of the article followed by a full stop

Give the name of the newspaper in italics, then the day it was printed. If you are supplying the URL, write 'available from' and give the full website address within chevrons (< >) followed by the date of access in square brackets

> Clark, D., O'Connor, M., Bangay, R. and Roche, R. (2009) Guardian's Quick Carbon Calculator. *Guardian* 21st October 2009, available from <http://www.guardian.co.uk/environment/interactive/2009/oct/20/guardian-quick-carbon-calculator> [25th October 2009]

A note about referencing articles

Some referencing styles instruct you to put single quote marks around article titles. Follow your recommended guidelines and if unsure, check with your tutor.

REFERENCING WEBSITES AND SIMILAR TYPES OF SOURCES

You usually need five pieces of information to reference a journal article. These are:

1 Author

2 Date

3 Webpage title

4 The full website address (URL)

5 The date of access.

Here is an example of how to reference a website:

Give the author or corporate author, the date in brackets, then the title of the webpage in italics. Write 'available from' and give the full website address within chevrons (< >) followed by the date of access in square brackets

➡️ Economics Network (2009) *Effective Writing and Referencing* available from <http://studyingeconomics.ac. uk/effective-writing/> [1st October 2009]

So, your entry for the list of references for a website should be as shown in Table 10.4:

Table 10.4 **Websites**

Corporate author	Date	Webpage title	Full website address (URL)	Date of access
Economics Network	(2009)	*Effective Writing and Referencing*	available from <http://studyingeconomics. ac.uk/effective-writing/>	[1st October 2009]

Audiovisual recordings as downloads

Downloaded sources are referenced in a similar way to a website. As there is such a range of different digital sources, the best advice to give is that you should adapt the formula for referencing websites using your own judgement, and as long as you are clear and consistent you will do a good job. If you have any concerns about referencing more unusual digital sources, ask your tutor for advice or seek guidance at your university library. Here is an example of how to reference a down-loaded audio source:

Give the corporate author, the date in brackets, then the title of the download in italics followed by a full stop, then the day and time it was broadcast. Write 'available from' and give the full website address within chevrons (< >) followed by the date of access in square brackets	*BBC Radio 4 (2009) St Thomas Aquinas. In Our Time with Melvyn Bragg.* 17th September 2009 9.00am, available from <http://www.bbc.co.uk/podcasts/series/iot> [23rd September 2009]

Audiovisual recordings (not downloaded)

Give the same author as you gave in your in-text citations and supply enough information for readers to find the source for themselves. Here is an example of how to reference a DVD giving the director as the author:

Give the surname and initial of the author, the date in brackets, then the title of the DVD in italics followed a full stop. Give the name of the company who produced the DVD	*Minghella, A. (2004) Cold Mountain.* Buena Vista Home Entertainment

Blogs

The formula for referencing blogs is similar to the method for referencing websites. Here is an example:

Give the surname and initial of the author, the date in brackets, then the title of the entry in italics, followed by a full stop, then the day and time it was added. Write 'available from' and give the full website address within chevrons (< >) followed by the date of access in square brackets	*Dwyer, J. (2009) Back to School: Tips for Teachers.* 18th September 2009 8.01pm available from <http://blog.facebook.com/> [22nd September 2009]

Online discussion fora and mailing lists

The formula for referencing discussion lists is similar to the method for referencing websites. Here is an example:

Give the surname and initial of the author, the date in brackets, then the title of the discussion thread in italics, followed by a full stop, then the day and time the comment was added. Write 'available from' and give the full website address within chevrons (< >) followed by the date of access in square brackets	*Harris, O. (2009) Teaching Practice.* 1st September 2009 5.30pm available from <eataw-conf@lists.hum.ku.dk> [22nd September 2009]

Personal communications

The formula for referencing personal communications is similar to the method for referencing websites. Here is an example of how to reference an email:

Give the surname and initial of the author, the date in brackets, then the subject of the email in italics, followed by a full stop, then the day and time it was added. Write 'available from' and give the full website address within chevrons (< >) followed by the date of access in square brackets

> Simms, P. (2010) *Enquiry re Invoice.* 5th January 2010 1.10pm available from <http://mail.live.com/default.aspx?&n=1011776457> [10th January 2010]

Lectures

The formula for referencing lectures is similar to the method for referencing a website, especially if you downloaded notes from your module web.

Should you borrow material from lectures?

It is not necessarily appropriate to cite and reference lectures in your academic writing because lecturers usually expect you to conduct independent research based on the ideas they share and the reading lists they distribute at lectures.

Here is an example of how to reference a lecture:

Give the surname and initial of the lecturer as author, the date in brackets, then the title of the lecture in italics followed by a full stop. Give the course code, a comma, then the day the lecture was delivered. Add a full stop then the university. Write 'available from' and give the full website address within chevrons (< >), followed by the date of access in square brackets (omit the URL and date of access if you did not download the lecture notes)

> Hobbs, R. (2010) *Case Law and Legal Writing.* Module 102 Law, 10th February 2010. Coventry University available from <http://legalwriting.ac.uk/caselaw-module102/> [1st February 2010]

Decisions about referencing

This section of Chapter 10 has explained how to reference using the Harvard style. It has covered the main points you need to know and recommended that you seek advice from your tutors or library specialists when you are unsure about any aspect of citing and referencing. It has indicated that there are times when you have to make decisions about how to reference sources. Base these decisions on the three following rules:

1 Be *clear* about where you have accessed sources

2 Be *consistent* in documenting sources in your list of references

3 Be *comprehensive* in giving all the details readers require to find sources for themselves.

SUMMARY

This chapter has explained how to use the Harvard style and has provided a wide range of examples (Deane 2009b). It has stressed the need to be clear and consistent as you acknowledge all the sources you use in your academic writing. It has emphasised that as you cite and reference unusual sources you need to use your own judgement and make decisions based on the advice of your tutors, library specialists, and your recommended referencing guidelines.

The main arguments in this chapter:

■ To cite sources you should give the author, date, and page number when appropriate

■ To reference sources you should learn the format for each type of source in your recommended referencing guidelines.

Assessment at university

How tests and examinations work

University assessment systems are complex and rather different from those used at school or college. This chapter clarifies the terminology involved and explains the rationale for different modes of assessment, while later chapters discuss how to tackle specific question types.

Key topics
- Forms of assessment
- Marking criteria and grading schemes
- Modules and progression
- Degree classifications and transcripts

Key terms
Aggregate mark   Class exam   Exam diet   External examiner   Finals
Formative assessment   Learning objective   Marking criteria
Oral exam   Peer assessment   Summative assessment   Transcript

Your university is an educational institution with a legal charter entitling it to award its own degrees. These degrees are granted on the basis of performance in exams and assessments, which may vary in character depending on subject and institution. As a result, each university has its own conventions regarding style of question, format of exams and marking criteria. No two universities are the same. It is essential that you take into account how the exam system operates in your own institution *before* you start revising.

Exam format

This should never come as a surprise to you as you should have checked up on it by looking at past papers and by confirming with lecturers that there have been no changes to the style of examination.

From Chapter 2 of *How to Succeed in Exams & Assessments*, 2/e. Kathleen McMillan and Jonathan Weyers. © Pearson Education Limited 2007, 2010 2011. All rights reserved.

Exam papers and diets may be structured in different ways, according to discipline. The design may reflect the different aspects of learning that your tutors wish to assess (**Ch 17** and **Ch 19**). For example, there may be a multiple-choice component that tests your surface knowledge across a wide range of topics, while an essay section may be included to test your deeper knowledge in fewer topics. Papers and questions may carry different weightings towards an aggregate mark.

Various levels of choice are given to reflect the nature of the field of study. In professional disciplines there may be a need to ensure you are knowledgeable in all areas, while in other subjects a certain amount of specialisation may be acceptable. Some exam papers are divided into sections, and you will be expected to answer one or more questions from the options within each of these. This format allows a limited amount of choice while ensuring that you have covered all major areas in your studies. You should take these aspects of exam paper design into account when arriving at a strategy for revision and exam-sitting (**Ch 15**).

● Forms of assessment

Each degree programme and every unit of teaching at university (usually called a 'module') will have a published set of aims and learning objectives or outcomes. Your performance in relation to these goals will be tested in various ways.

- **Formative assessments** are primarily designed to give you feedback on the quality of your answers. In some instances these are known as 'class exams'. They generally do not count towards your final module assessment, although sometimes a small proportion of marks will carry forward as an incentive to perform well.

- **Summative assessments** count directly towards a module or degree assessment. Many summative exams are held as formal invigilated tests where you work in isolation. These may be known as degree exams and, in the honours year, in some institutions, as 'finals'. These exams may comprise several sittings or papers, perhaps covering different aspects of the course, and often lasting for two or three hours each. The collective set of exams is sometimes known as an exam diet.

In some cases, in-course work will count towards degree exams (continuous assessment). This can take the form of essays, projects, and special exercises like problem-based learning. However, the majority of marks are usually devoted to formal invigilated exams where the possibility of collaboration, plagiarism and impersonation are limited, and you will be expected to perform alone under a certain amount of time pressure.

Problem-based learning (PBL)

This is a form of learning where you are asked to investigate a specific problem, usually related to a real-life professional situation, which may be open-ended in nature (that is, not necessarily having a 'right answer'). You may be part of a small team asked to consider the problem, research the underlying theory and practice that might lead to a response, and arrive at a practical solution. Assessment of the exercise will focus not only on the solution you arrive at, but also on the way in which you arrive at it, so here process is often at least as important as the product. There may be group- and peer-assessment elements that contribute to your grade.

● Marking criteria and grading schemes

Who marks your papers? How do they do it? Often students are unsure about this. The norm is for papers to be graded by the person who delivered the lectures, tutorials or practical classes. With large classes, alternative mechanisms may be employed:

- the marking may be spread out among several tutors;
- especially in multiple-choice papers, the marking may be automated;
- where teamwork is involved, peer assessment may take place.

Peer assessment

This is where the members of a study team are asked to assign a mark to each other's performance. This might take account, for example, of the effort put in, the conduct in the assigned team role(s), and contribution to the final outcome. Clear guidance is always given about how you should assign marks. One point of this method is to help students become more aware of how work is assessed by academic staff.

Each university will publish assessment scales, usually in handbooks and/or websites. Some operate to a familiar system of banded percentages, often related to honours degree classifications, while others adopt a different form of band 'descriptors'. Find out which system applies in your case and consult the general marking criteria used to assign work in each band. This will give you a better idea of the standard of work needed to produce a specific grade, and may help you to understand feedback.

To maintain standards and ensure fairness, several systems operate. For example:

- there may be an explicit marking scheme that allocates a proportion of the total to different aspects of your answer;
- double- or triple-marking may take place and if the grades awarded differ, then the answer may be scrutinised more closely, possibly by a external examiner;
- papers are usually marked anonymously, so the marker does not know whose answer they are grading;
- the external marker will confirm the overall standard and may inspect some papers, particularly those falling at the division between honours grades or on the pass/fail boundary;
- accreditation bodies in the professions may be involved in the examination process, and some answer papers may be marked by external assessors appointed by these bodies rather than by university staff.

 External examiners

These are appointed by the university to ensure standards are maintained and that the assessment is fair. They are usually noted academics in the field, with wide experience of examining. They review the exam question papers in advance and will generally look closely at a representative selection of written papers and project work. For finals, they may interview students in an oral, to ensure that spoken responses meet the standard of the written answers, and to arrive at a judgement on borderline cases.

● Modules and progression

Modular systems of study at university have been developed for several reasons:

- they allow greater flexibility in subject choice;
- they can efficiently accommodate students studying different degree paths;
- they make it easier for students to transfer between courses and institutions;
- they break up studies into 'bite-sized' elements and allow exams to be spread out more evenly over the academic year.

The set of modules that make up a degree programme are usually selected to build on each other in a complementary way, and to allow you to develop skills that you can take forward to the next level of study. Therefore, you should avoid:

- dodging seemingly difficult or unattractive subjects;
- 'closing the book' on a subject once it has been assessed; or
- limiting your degree options.

Modules are usually assessed in a summative end-of-module exam, perhaps with a component from in-course assessment. In some subjects, borderline cases are given an extra oral exam. If you fail the end-of-module exam (and any oral), a resit may be possible. Resits usually take place towards the end of the summer vacation. The result is usually based solely on your performance in the resit exam.

At the end of each academic year, and after any resits, you will be required to fulfil certain progression criteria that allow you to pass on to the next level of study. These criteria are normally published in course handbooks. If you fail to satisfy the criteria, you may need to resit the whole year or even to leave the university. Sometimes you may be asked to 'carry' specific modules: that is, study them again in addition to the normal quota for your next year of study. Some institutions may place a condition on your re-entry, for example, achieving a certain level of marks or passing a prescribed number of modules in order to progress. This would normally be discussed with your adviser/director of studies.

Appeals against termination of studies

Students' studies may be terminated for one of several reasons, but most commonly failure to meet attendance or progression criteria. Occasionally, termination will be enforced due to disciplinary reasons, for example, in a case of plagiarism. Students will normally be offered a chance to appeal and will be expected to produce evidence of any extenuating circumstances, such as medical certificates, or notes from support service personnel. Such students may also wish to ask tutors to support their application where the tutor is aware of their personal situation.

Degree classifications and transcripts

Students with superior entry qualifications or experience may join university at different levels. There are also a range of exit awards – certificates, diplomas and ordinary degrees. However, the majority of students now enter at level 1, and study for an honours degree. This encompasses three years of study in England, Wales and Northern Ireland, and four years in Scotland. Credit will normally be given for years of study carried out abroad or in work placement, according to specific schemes operated by your university. This includes participation in European Community schemes such as ERASMUS or LINGUA (see **http://europa.eu.int/index_en.htm**).

Sometimes entry into the final honours year is competitive, based on grades in earlier years. Some universities operate a junior honours year, which means being accepted into an honours stream at an earlier stage and with special module options.

Nearly all universities follow the same honours degrees grading system, which is, in descending order:

- first class (a 'first');
- upper second class (a two-one or 2:1);
- lower second class (a two-two or 2:2);
- third class (a 'third');
- unclassified.

(Certain universities do not differentiate the second class divisions.)

In some institutions, these classifications will take into account all grades you have obtained during your university career; sometimes only those in junior and senior honours years; and in the majority, only grades obtained in the finals. This makes the finals critical, especially as there are no resits for them.

Once your degree classification has been decided by the examination committee or board, and moderated by the external examiner, it will be passed for ratification to the university's senate or equivalent body for academic legislation. During this period you will technically be a graduand, until your degree is conferred at the graduation ceremony. At this time you will receive your degree certificate and be entitled to wear a specifically coloured hood for your gown that denotes your degree and institution.

Job prospects with different degrees

In a competitive job market, your chances of being considered for a position may depend on your degree classification, but employers also take into account other personal qualities and experience. Research positions that involve reading for a higher degree, such as an MSc or PhD, usually require a first or 2:1.

Employers will usually ask to see your diploma for confirmation of your degree and may contact the university to confirm your qualification and obtain a copy of your transcript. This document shows your performance in *all* assessments throughout your career at the university.

Practical tips for understanding the assessment system

Ask senior students about the exam system. They may have useful tips and advice to pass on.

Find out where essential information is recorded. This could be in a combination of handbooks and web-based resources.

If you don't understand any aspect of the assessment system, ask course administrators or tutors. Knowing how the system works is important and can affect your performance.

Notify your institution of any disability

If you have a disability, you should make the institution aware of this. You may have special concessions in exams, for example, using the services of a scribe, being allowed extra time, or having exam question papers printed in large print for you. Appropriate entitlements take time to arrange and you must ensure that arrangements are in place well before the exam date. Contact your department and disability support service for guidance.

GO And now . . .

2.1 Carry out the necessary research to ensure you know how your university's exam system works for your intended degree. You should find out about:

- course and degree programme aims;
- learning objectives or outcomes;
- the format of assessments and proportion of in-course and final exam elements;
- timing of exam diets;
- assessment or marking criteria;
- the grading scheme;
- weighting of exam components;
- progression criteria.

2.2 Find out about in-course assessments and how they will contribute to your module or degree grade. Your course handbooks will normally include this information. Marks for in-course work can often be influenced by the amount of work you put in, so they can be a good way of ensuring you create a strong platform to perform well in summative exams. Some courses include an element relating to attendance as part of the assessment.

2.3 Examine past exam papers in your subjects to investigate how they are constructed. This will allow you to see whether there are subdivisions, restrictions or other features that might influence your revision or exam strategies.

Newcastle University's Official Geography Assessment Criteria (Stage 1)

Standards / Mark	0-29	30-39	40-49	50-59	60-69	70-79	80-100
Classification / Type of Assessment	**Bad fail**	**Marginal fail**	**Basic**	**Good**	**Very Good**	**Excellent**	**Outstanding**
Assessed Essays	Highly inaccurate. Little evidence of having studied the course. No argument. No critical analysis. No evidence of reading or making use of relevant evidence. Weak structure. Writing lacks clarity.	Errors in understanding. Evidence of having studied only a very narrow range of material, less than that provided. Little or no reference to key sources, terms, debates or evidence.	Evidence of having studied the course material. Some accurate elements. Largely descriptive with little by way of an argument. Uses a simple but appropriate structure. Clearly written in places but lacking fluency.	Evidence of having studied some material on the reading list beyond that provided. Reasonable level of accuracy shown. Small amount of critical analysis. Clearly expressed in places but lacking sophistication.	Evidence of having studied a wide range of material. Able to apply directly relevant. Good understanding of a majority of the concepts, terms and debates. Uses a good structure to generate an argument. Some critical analysis. Generally well expressed and quite fluent.	Evidence of having studied material beyond that recommended for the module. Broad and occasionally deep understanding of a complex concepts, terms and debates. Coherently structured. Well developed argument. Skilled critical analysis. Clearly expressed.	Ambitious in range of well chosen material, venturing well beyond what would normally be expected at stage one. A convincing argument showing advanced skills of critical and independent thinking. Coherently structured and elegantly written. Sophisticated.
Oral/Group Presentations	Little evidence of preparation or understanding. Poor time-keeping. Lacks structure. Lacks reference to relevant material.	Some evidence of preparation but limited understanding. Lacking clarity and relevance. Limited use of evidence. Poor ability to engage the audience.	Evidence of preparation and basic competence in structure and delivery. Remains largely descriptive with very little argument or critical comment.	Good evidence of having prepared some relevant material beyond that provided. Good time-management and use of an appropriate structure. Some understanding and linkage of concepts.	Very well prepared. Good selection of relevant material. Good understanding of a majority of the material. Able to deliver a well-paced, quite engaging presentation.	Excellent preparation. Able to draw on relevant material from outside the course. Broad and occasionally deep understanding of material. A presentation which is convincing and engaging.	Ambitious and innovative use of relevant material from outside the course. Broad and deep understanding of material. An engaging presentation which is authoritative and includes original ideas.
Assessed Practical/ Empirical Project	Very little technical skill applied. Very poor presentation. Very limited evidence used. Little or no evidence of having studied essential material.	Basic technical competence in a small number of simple areas. Little use of evidence and limited understanding of essential concepts.	Demonstrating basic technical competence in some areas and some understanding of basic concepts. Some use of relevant evidence.	Demonstrating a reasonable level of technical competence and generally accurate understanding. Appropriate use of a reasonable range of evidence. A simple argument which is clearly presented.	Demonstrating a good level of technical competence and good overall understanding. Uses a wide range of appropriate evidence. A reasonably complex argument which is well presented.	Demonstrating a very high level of technical competence. Evidence of understanding and occasionally deep understanding. Wide range of well chosen evidence well beyond that provided.	Demonstrating a very high level of technical competence. Evidence of understanding and analytic skills beyond that normally expected at stage one. Able to draw on relevant evidence from outside the course to support a complex argument
Unseen Exam	Highly inaccurate. Failure to read and follow the exam question(s) and/or failure to complete all the questions required. Very limited reference to the material relevant to the exam questions.	Failure to understand and follow the exam questions/ instructions. Evidence of having studied a very narrow range of material.	Basic ability to recall and communicate some accurate material and relevant ideas. Evidence of having studied the essential materials provided. A simple argument	Largely accurate and relevant to the question. Evidence of having studied some material beyond the essential. A simple argument supported by some critical analysis in places.	Good level of accuracy and good use of material which is directly relevant to the question. Evidence of having studied a wide range of material. A quite well developed argument supported by some critical analysis.	A high level of accuracy and excellent use of a wide range of relevant and quite advanced material. Some good critical analysis and reasonably complex argument. An ability to link ideas and think independently.	A high level of accuracy and reference to material and ideas well beyond that considered usual at stage one. A compelling argument showing independent and critical thinking. Able to synthesise and link ideas.

107

Newcastle University's Official Geography Assessment Criteria (Stages 2 and 3)

Standards / Mark	0-29	30-39	40-49	50-59	60-69	70-79	80-100
Class	**Bad fail**	**Marginal fail**	**Third**	**Lower Second**	**Upper Second**	**First**	**Outstanding First**
Assessment Type							
Dissertation	A thesis which displays **serious lack of understanding** of the principles of the subject. Contains major errors, serious deficiencies in knowledge, expression and organisation; poor use of English, substantial omissions and irrelevancies. No attempt to cite and/or use sources	Limited or misdirected analysis showing **little appreciation of context** or understanding of appropriate methods and techniques. Poorly structured. Conclusions unsupported by previous analysis. A thesis which includes significant errors and irrelevancies which raises doubts about the candidate's grasp of the essentials of the subject. Very poor attempt to cite sources	Limited or superficial analysis with errors in application or interpretation, but **broadly appropriate choice of methods and techniques.** Limited review of relevant literature. Presented in an adequate framework. Uncritical coverage of debates and issues, but with adequate comprehension of some basic facts and principles. Little evidence of reading, and limited understanding of the question. Relatively weak skills of planning and argument construction; weak grasp of concepts. Some attempt to cite sources.	Limited or superficial analysis with some use of appropriate methods and techniques. Brief review of relevant literature with limited evidence of additional, independent study and a lack of independent thought. **Uneven,** showing strength in some areas but weaknesses in others. Presented in an adequate framework. Weaknesses may include a **lack of critical analysis,** and a tendency to be descriptive; lack of structure, poor expression. Adequate but not accurate citation of sources.	**Thorough investigation** of research topic using appropriate methods and techniques supported by thorough review of relevant literature and presented in a well structured framework. A **well-organised,** detailed and structured thesis showing a thorough understanding of the subject as taught, and evidence of additional study. Competence in most areas, but may also **display excellence in others. Makes a serious attempt to engage with the question set.** Sources cited accurately.	**Perceptive analysis** using considered choice of research methods and techniques, supported by **critical review of relevant literature** and presented in a well structured framework. An excellent thesis displaying **evidence of independent thought,** initiative and intellectual rigour. Empirical fieldwork is not a requirement for an award in this classification.	In addition to criteria under 70-79%, work which includes **substantial evidence of originality and** independent thought, exceptional for an undergraduate. Ambitious in scope, it will display **sophisticated handling of critical and complex issues.** In exceptional circumstances, a mark of 90% or above could be awarded for work which is considered suitable for academic publication. Ability to engage with cutting edge scholarship. Sources cited thoroughly and accurately.
Assessed Essays	A discussion which displays **serious lack of understanding** of the principles of the subject. Contains **major errors,** serious deficiencies in knowledge, expression and organisation; poor use of English, **substantial omissions and irrelevances.** No attempt to cite and/or use sources	**Little or misdirected effort.** Shallow and poorly presented. Lacking in **conclusions or conclusions incorrect.** A discussion which includes significant errors and irrelevances which raises doubts about the candidate's grasp of the essentials of the subject. Very poor attempt to cite sources	Very basic approach to a narrow or misguided selection of material. Lacking in background or **flawed in argument.** Uncritical coverage of debates and issues, but with **adequate comprehension** of some basic facts and principles. **Little evidence of reading,** and limited understanding of the question. Relatively weak skills of planning and argument construction; **weak grasp of concepts.** Some attempt to cite sources.	Pedestrian treatment. A "correct" answer **based largely on lecture material** with limited evidence of additional, independent study and a lack of independent thought. **Uneven,** showing strength in some areas but weaknesses in others. Some small errors allowed. Weaknesses may include a **lack of critical analysis,** and a tendency to be descriptive; lack of structure; **poor expression.** Adequate but not accurate citation of sources.	Thorough clear treatment; **shows understanding of** arguments and context. A **well-organised,** detailed and structured discussion showing a thorough understanding of the subject as taught, and **evidence of additional study.** Competence in most areas, but may also display excellence in others. Makes a **serious attempt to engage with the question set.** Sources cited accurately.	**Perceptive** focused use of an appropriate breadth and good **depth of** material with attention to salient detail. Evidence of **critical insight and** depth of analytical understanding required. An excellent answer displaying evidence of **independent thought,** initiative and intellectual rigour.	In addition to criteria under 70-79%, work which includes substantial evidence of originality and **independent thought,** exceptional for an undergraduate. Ambitious in scope, it will display **sophisticated** handling of critical and complex issues. In exceptional circumstances, a mark of 90% or above could be awarded for work which is considered suitable for academic publication. Ability to engage with cutting edge scholarship. Sources cited thoroughly and accurately.

Stage 2 and 3 Assessment Criteria Continued

Standards / Mark	0-29	30-39	40-49	50-59	60-69	70-79	80-100
Class	**Bad fail**	**Marginal fail**	**Third**	**Lower Second**	**Upper Second**	**First**	**Outstanding First**
Assessment Type							
Oral/Group Presentations	Little evidence of preparation or understanding. Poor time-keeping. Lacks structure. Lacks reference to relevant material.	Some evidence of preparation but limited understanding. Lacking clarity and relevance. Limited use of evidence. Poor ability to engage the audience.	Evidence of preparation and basic competence in structure and delivery. Remains largely descriptive with very little argument or critical comment.	Good evidence of having prepared some relevant material beyond that provided. Good time-management and use of an appropriate structure. Some understanding and linkage of concepts.	Very well prepared. Good selection of relevant material. Good understanding of a majority of the material. Able to deliver a well-paced, quite engaging presentation.	Excellent preparation. Able to draw on relevant material from outside the course. Broad and occasionally deep understanding of material. A presentation which is convincing and engaging.	Ambitious and innovative use of relevant material from outside the course. Broad and deep understanding of material. An engaging presentation which is authoritative and includes original ideas.
Empirical Project	A project which displays serious **lack of understanding** of the principles of the subject. Contains **major errors,** serious deficiencies in knowledge, expression and organisation; poor use of English, substantial omissions and irrelevances. No attempt to cite and/or use sources.	**Poor understanding** of relevant concepts, techniques and results, with **significant errors** in understanding or application. A project which includes significant errors and irrelevancies which raises doubts about the candidate's grasp of the essentials of the subject. Very poor attempt to cite sources	Demonstrating **basic technical competence** in some areas and some understanding of basic concepts but with basic errors in understanding or application in some areas. **Uncritical** coverage of debates and issues, but with adequate comprehension of some basic facts and principles. Little evidence of reading, and limited understanding of the question. Relatively weak skills of planning and argument construction; weak grasp of concepts. Some attempt to cite sources.	**Broad understanding** of relevant concepts, techniques and results but with some errors in understanding or application. Weaknesses may include a lack of critical analysis, and a **tendency to be descriptive;** lack of structure; poor expression. Adequate but not accurate citation of sources.	Good overall understanding of relevant concepts, techniques and results, but with some minor errors in understanding or application. A well-organised, detailed and structured project showing **a thorough understanding of the subject as taught,** and evidence of additional study. **Competence in most areas,** but may also display excellence in others. Makes a serious attempt to engage with the question set. Sources cited accurately.	Demonstrating a very **high level of technical competence.** Coherent understanding of relevant concepts, techniques and results, applied appropriately to the problem. An excellent project displaying **evidence of independent thought,** initiative and intellectual rigour.	**Ambitious in range of material used** and showing a very high level of technical competence and accuracy. Wide range of well chosen **evidence skilfully and confidently applied** to complex issues. Evidence of independent and original thinking and synthesis. Sources cited thoroughly and accurately. Ability to **engage with cutting edge scholarship.** In exceptional circumstances, a mark of 90% or above could be worthy of dissemination.
Unseen Exam	Highly inaccurate. Failure to read and follow the exam question(s) and/or failure to complete all the questions required. Very limited reference to the material relevant to the exam questions.	Failure to understand and follow the exam questions/ instructions. Evidence of having studied a very narrow range of material.	Basic ability to recall and communicate some accurate material and relevant ideas. Evidence of having studied the essential materials provided. A simple argument.	Largely accurate and relevant to the question. Evidence of having studied some material beyond the essential. A simple argument supported by some critical analysis in places.	Perceptive treatment of the issues. A well-organised, detailed and logical answer showing a thorough understanding of the subject as taught, and evidence of additional study. General competence, excellence in places. A serious attempt to engage with the question set. Sources cited accurately.	Perceptive focused use of an appropriate breadth and good depth of material with attention to salient detail. Evidence of critical insight and depth of analytical understanding required. An excellent answer displaying evidence of independent thought, initiative and intellectual rigour.	In addition to criteria under 70-79%, work which includes substantial evidence of originality and independent thought, exceptional for an undergraduate. A compelling argument showing critical analysis. Able to synthesise and link ideas. Ability to engage with cutting edge scholarship.

109

Exploiting feedback

How to understand and learn from what lecturers write on your work

When you receive back assessed work and exam scripts, these may be annotated by the marker or provided in a standard feedback sheet. It is essential that you learn from these comments if you want to improve. This chapter outlines some common annotations and describes how you should react to them.

Key topics
- Types of feedback
- Examples of feedback comments and what they mean

Key terms
Formative assessment   Summative assessment

There are two principal types of assessment at university: formative and summative. Formative assessments are those in which the grade received does not contribute to your end-of-module mark, or contributes relatively little, while giving you an indication of the standard of your work. It is often accompanied by a feedback sheet or comments written on the script. Summative assessments contribute directly to your final module mark and include things such as end-of-term/semester exams, project reports or essay submissions.

● Types of feedback

The simplest pointer from any type of assessment is the grade you receive; if good, you know that you have reached the expected standard; if poor, you know that you should try to improve.

If you feel unsure about the grading system or what standard is expected at each grading level, your course, school or faculty handbooks will probably include a description of marking or assessment criteria that explain this.

From Chapter 10 of *How to Succeed in Exams & Assessments*, 2/e. Kathleen McMillan and Jonathan Weyers. © Pearson Education Limited 2007, 2010 2011. All rights reserved.

How well are you performing?

The answer, of course, depends on your goals and expectations, but also on your understanding of degree classifications and their significance. Even in early levels of study, it may be worth relating percentage marks or other forms of grades (descriptors) to the standard degree classes – first, upper second, lower second, third and unclassified. Certain career and advanced degree opportunities will only be open to those with higher-level qualifications, and you should try to gain an understanding of how this operates in your field of study and likely career destination. In this way you will know the targets you need to hit in order to achieve these goals.

Written feedback may be provided on your assessed work. This will often take the form of handwritten comments on your text, and a summary commenting on your work or justifying why it received the mark it did. Sometimes the feedback will be provided separately from your submission so that other markers are not influenced by it.

Some feedback may be oral and informal, for example, a demonstrator's comment given as you work in a practical, or an observation on your contribution during a tutorial. If you feel uncertain about why your work has received the grade it did, or why a particular comment was provided, you may be able to arrange a meeting with the person who assessed your work. Normally they will be happy to provide further oral explanations. However, do not attempt to haggle over your marks, other than to point out politely if part of your work does not appear to have been marked at all, or part marks appear to have been added up wrongly.

Always read your feedback

You will want to do your best, so make a point of reading feedback carefully. Regardless of your grade, all comments in your feedback should give you constructive direction for later efforts and are designed to help you to develop the structure and style of your work, as well as encourage you to develop a deeper understanding of the topic. Where students ignore points, especially those about presentation or structure, then they may find themselves heavily penalised in later submissions.

● Examples of feedback comments and what they mean

Different lecturers use different terms to express similar meanings, and because they mark quickly, their handwritten comments are sometimes untidy and may be difficult to interpret. This means that you may need help in deciphering their meaning. Table 10.1 illustrates feedback comments that are frequently made and explains how you should react to obtain better grades in future. If a particular comment or mark does not make sense to you after reading these tables, then you may wish to approach the marker for an explanation.

Practical tips for dealing with feedback

Be mentally prepared to learn from the views of your tutors. You may initially feel that feedback is unfair, harsh or that it misunderstands the approach you were trying to take to the question. A natural reaction might be to dismiss many of the comments. However, you should recognise that tutors probably have a much deeper understanding of the topic than you, and concede that if you want to do well in a subject then you need to gain a better understanding of what makes a good answer from the academic's point of view.

Always make sure you understand the feedback. Check with fellow students or with the lecturers involved if you cannot read the comment or do not understand why it has been made.

React constructively to *all* your feedback. Make a note of common or repeated errors, even in peripheral topics, so that you can avoid them in later assignments.

Get to know the standard proof-reading symbols and the abbreviations used by your tutors. Lecturers and tutors use a variety of words and symbols to suggest corrections and modifications. Most symbols will be standard ones used in editing (for example, ≡ placed under a letter means that it should be capitalised). If you find you cannot understand them, consult one of the standard texts for readers and compositors (for example, *Hart's Rules*, Ritter, 2005).

Table 10.1 **Common types of feedback annotation and how to act in response.** Comments in the margin may be accompanied by underlining of word(s), circling of phrases, sentences or paragraphs.

Types of comment and typical examples	Meaning and potential remedial action
Regarding content	
Relevance Relevance? Importance? Value of example? So?	An example or quotation may not be apt, or you may not have explained its relevance. Think about the logic of your narrative or argument and whether there is a mismatch as implied, or whether you could add further explanation; choose a more appropriate example or quote.
Detail Give more information Example? Too much detail/waffle/padding	You are expected to flesh out your answer with more detail or an example to illustrate your point; or, conversely, you may have provided too much information. It may be that your work lacks substance and you appear to have compensated by putting in too much description rather than analysis, for example.
Specific factual comment or comment on your approach You could have included . . . What about . . . ? Why didn't you . . . ?	Depends on context, but it should be obvious what is required to accommodate the comment.
Expressions of approval Good! Excellent! ✓ (may be repeated)	You got this right or chose a good example. Keep up the good work!
Expressions of disapproval Poor Weak No! ✗ (may be repeated)	Sometimes obvious, but may not be clear. The implication is that your example's logic could be improved.
Regarding structure	
Fault in logic or argument Logic! Non sequitur (does not follow)	Your argument or line of logic is faulty. This may require quite radical changes to your approach to the topic.
Failure to introduce topic clearly Where are you going with this? Unclear	What is your understanding of the task? What parameters will confine your response? How do you intend to tackle the subject?

Table 10.1 continued

Types of comment and typical examples	Meaning and potential remedial action
Failure to construct a logical discussion Imbalanced discussion Weak on pros and cons	When you have to compare and contrast in any way, then it is important that you give each element in your discussion equal coverage.
Failure to conclude essay clearly So what? Conclusion	You have to leave a 'take-home message' that sums up the most salient features of your writing and you should not include new material in this section. This is to demonstrate your ability to think critically and define the key aspects.
Heavy dependency on quotations Watch out for over-quotation Too many quotations	There is a real danger of plagiarism if you include too many direct quotations from text. However, in a subject like English literature or law, quotation may be a key characteristic of writing. In this case, quotation is permitted, provided that it is supported by critical comment.
Move text Loops and arrows	Suggestion for changing order of text, usually to enhance the flow or logic.
Regarding presentation	
Minor proofing errors sp. (spelling) Λ (insert material here) ⌐ (break paragraph here) ⁊ (delete this material)	A (minor) correction is required.
Citations Reference (required) Reference or bibliography list omitted Ref!	You have not supported evidence, argument or quotation with a reference to the original source. This is important in academic work and if you fail to do it, you may be considered guilty of plagiarism. If you omit a reference list, this will lose you marks as it implies a totally unsourced piece of writing.
Tidiness Illegible! Can't read	Your handwriting on the exam script may be difficult to decipher.
Failure to follow recommended format Please follow departmental template for reports Order!	If the department or school provides a template for the submission of reports, then you must follow it. If you don't, then you may lose marks.

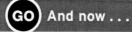

And now . . .

10.1 Check out your department, school or faculty's marking criteria. As explained above, these may help you interpret feedback and understand how to reach the standard you want to achieve.

10.2 Decide what to do about feedback comments you frequently receive. For instance, do lecturers always comment about your spelling or grammar; or suggest you should use more examples; or ask for more citations to be included? You might consider consulting your university's academic skills unit whose learning specialists may be able to help you improve in the necessary areas.

10.3 Learn to criticise drafts of your own work. This is equivalent to giving feedback to yourself and is an essential academic skill. Annotate drafts of your own work - this is an important way to refine it and improve its quality.

Succeeding in exams and assessments

Understanding the processes involved in revision and exam-sitting

This book aims to support students who want to succeed in university exams. Achieving this goal will be much easier if you start with a mental picture of the different processes involved in revision and exam-sitting and use this information to arrive at a strategy to guide your efforts.

Key topics
- Information gathering
- Information processing
- Information retrieval and delivery

Key terms
Autonomous learner   Displacement activity   Learning objectives
Learning outcomes   Learning styles   Marking criteria

If you wish to revise effectively, it is crucial that you know what you are trying to accomplish. One way of gaining this understanding is to divide the revision and exam-sitting process into components and look at what you need to achieve at each stage. The process is essentially about managing information – the facts and understanding gained during your course – and can be separated into three main elements:

- information gathering;
- information processing; and
- information retrieval and delivery.

If you do the right things in each of these phases you will greatly increase your chances of achieving excellent grades.

From Chapter 1 of *How to Succeed in Exams & Assessments*, 2/e. Kathleen McMillan and Jonathan Weyers. © Pearson Education Limited 2007, 2010 2011. All rights reserved.

● Information gathering

As a result of attending lectures, tutorials or practicals, and from carrying out additional background reading, you will have access to a large amount of information in the form of lecture notes, handouts, printouts (for example, PowerPoint presentations), tutorial or practical notes, textbooks, notes from textbooks and other sources, coursework you may have carried out, and online material. You will probably be able to consult two other vital resources: learning objectives (or learning outcomes) and past exam papers. You should not forget to consult any feedback that you received on coursework assignments as this may give you useful direction on areas of weakness or aspects that require more attention on your part.

In this phase of revision your aim is to ensure that you have copies of all that you require close to hand, and to make sure that it is well organised so that you can consult what you need, quickly:

❏ Check that you have all the lecture notes and make arrangements to download or copy them, if you do not have these things in place.

❏ File your notes in sequence.

❏ Buy or borrow the textbooks that support your course (check the reading list in the course handbook). Alternatively, look these up in your library catalogue and place reservations on them if they are available only on limited access.

❏ Gather together all other materials that might be relevant, such as completed coursework with feedback.

❏ Bookmark any online resources that you might be expected to consult.

❏ Obtain copies of past papers and model answers, if available.

❏ Find out where the learning objectives or outcomes are published (for example, in the course handbook), and make a copy of them.

❏ Look in your course handbook for any special guidance notes on the exam and its format.

 Managing the time taken for information gathering

You must not let the information gathering phase take up too much of your revision time - recognise that it can be a displacement activity and limit the time you allocate to it within your revision timetable (Ch 8).

There are many potential sources of information about any topic, and a key aspect of your early university education is that you are guided by your tutors as to what is important and reliable, and what is not. Students at higher levels are expected to carry out elements of this task for themselves, as autonomous learners. Working out exactly how much and what kind of extra information you require is closely linked to how you will need to process it.

What is autonomous learning?

At university, you are normally expected to frame your own learning within the context of your course. This self-management is often referred to as 'autonomy' and means that you need to be able to work on your own, defining the knowledge and understanding that you need to achieve goals, solve problems and create new outcomes. The ability to learn autonomously develops over time. As you become more experienced as a student, you will recognise and develop skills and approaches that will make you an independent learner.

● Information processing

This revision phase involves analysing and manipulating the material you have gathered, with the learning objectives and past exam papers in mind. The principle is not to study passively, for example, by reading through the written material, but to try to do something active, to help you to memorise it (**Ch 11** and **Ch 12**).

Thinking about thinking

It is important to recognise that university teaching is not solely about information transfer where you just accumulate information and memorise a series of facts from lectures and other source material. You must be able *use* information. In short, you must develop skills in critical thinking. The facts are still required, but it is what you do with them - the critical thinking - in response to the exam or assessment instruction that is important (**Ch 15**). Benjamin Bloom, a noted educational psychologist, and colleagues, identified six different stages involved in the acquisition of learning and the process of thinking. These are popularly listed as:

- Knowledge
- Comprehension
- Application
- Analysis
- Synthesis
- Evaluation

Bloom *et al.* (1956) showed that students were expected to progress through this scale of thought-processing during their studies (Table 1.1). Looking at this table, you may recognise that your school or college work mainly focussed on knowledge, comprehension and application, while your university tutors tend to expect more in terms of analysis, synthesis and evaluation. These expectations are sometimes closely linked to the instruction words used in exam questions. Table 1.1 provides a few examples. However, take care when interpreting these instructions, as processes and tasks may mean different things in different subjects. For example, while 'description'

Table 1.1 **A classification of learning objectives derived from the work of Benjamin Bloom and colleagues (1956)**

Taxonomy of learning objectives (in ascending order of difficulty)	Typical question instructions
Knowledge. If you know a fact, you have it at your disposal and can *recall* or *recognise* it. This does not mean you necessarily understand it at a higher level	• Define • Describe • Identify
Comprehension. To comprehend a fact means that you *understand* what it means	• Contrast • Discuss • Interpret
Application. To apply a fact means that you can *put it to use*	• Demonstrate • Calculate • Illustrate
Analysis. To analyse information means that you are able to *break it down into parts* and show how these components *fit together*	• Analyse • Explain • Compare
Synthesis. To synthesise, you need to be able to *extract relevant facts* from a body of knowledge and use these to *address an issue in a novel way* or *create something new*	• Compose • Create • Integrate
Evaluation. If you evaluate information, you *arrive at a judgement* based on its importance relative to the topic being addressed	• Recommend • Support • Draw a conclusion

might imply a lower-level activity in the arts, it might involve high-level skills in subjects such as architecture.

When you analyse the instructions used in exam questions, you should take into account what type of thinking process the examiner has asked you to carry out, and try your best to reach the required level.

Thinking about learning

When starting out at university, it may be useful to consider or reconsider the ways in which you learn best. This is a personal matter: people differ greatly in their preferences for processing and retrieving information. For some students, developing an understanding of this aspect of their character makes a huge difference to their levels of attainment. Chapter 4 considers various types of learning personality, different methods of diagnosing your learning style, and the best ways of approaching study and revision once you know where your learning preferences lie.

Understanding the university exam system

Your department or school will provide plenty of helpful information about assessment. You can find it in course or programme handbooks, printed or online. Accessing this material will help you process the course material and your notes appropriately.

- **Learning objectives/outcomes.** These signify what your tutors believe you should be able to accomplish after participating in the different parts of the syllabus and carrying out the further studies they have recommended. They are a vital resource to you when revising, as they will help you interpret the course materials correctly and gain clues about the sorts of exam questions that will be set (**Ch 9**).

Keys to successful information processing

As part of an approach based on active revision, you will probably wish to reduce or 'distil' the notes you have made (**Ch 11**). This can only be done effectively with a clear idea of the sort of questions that will be asked and an indication of the depth at which you will be expected to deal with the material. In part, this information can be obtained by studying the learning objectives or outcomes and past exam papers.

- **Design of exam papers.** To process information effectively as part of your revision, it is essential to look at past papers. These will be valuable in three respects:
  - **Type of exam.** Tutors use different forms of assessment, depending on which aspects of your learning they wish to evaluate (**Ch 17** and **Ch 21**). If you understand why they have chosen a particular form, you can adjust your revision strategy to take this into account.
  - **Style of questions.** The ways in which you will be expected to process the information you have collated can be deduced from the style of questions in past papers. For example, you can figure out the scope of knowledge and depth of understanding that will be expected by relating each question to the learning objectives and the syllabus as taught (**Ch 9**).
  - **Weighting of marks.** Information about the proportion of marks allocated to different questions or sections of a paper will give you an indication of the effort you should put into each topic within your revision timetable (and during the exam). As a rough guide, the proportion of time spent revising, or answering specific questions in exams, should match the proportion of marks allocated. However, you may wish to adjust this balance if a particular topic is difficult for you (**Ch 8** and **Ch 15**).

If past papers are not available in any of your subjects, you should consider meeting with others in your class to see if, together, you can come up with ideas about potential questions and styles of question (**Ch 6** and **Ch 9**).

 Beware of changes to the syllabus or to the construction of exam papers

It is worth remembering that courses may change over time, as can the staff teaching them. This can have a considerable impact on content and the course structure. These should be flagged to you within the course handbook, or by tutors, but it might be worth confirming with the course leader or departmental administrator if you sense a mismatch between the syllabus as taught and the learning objectives or question papers. The same applies to checking whether you can assume that this year's exam papers will be constructed in the same way as in previous years.

- **Marking criteria.** These statements indicate the levels of attainment that tutors expect for different grades (**Ch 2**). They are the benchmarks for assessing the evidence of your learning, as shown in your responses to assessments and exams. The marking criteria are useful to look at before you start revising: allied with an understanding of Table 1.1, they will give you a better feel for how deep your understanding should be and for the standards that apply to your work.

Using feedback from past exams and assessment

Feedback you have received about your previous exam and assessment performances (**Ch 10**) should affect how you carry out information processing during revision. For example, this might indicate that your answers have lacked relevance or sufficient depth. You should therefore adjust your approach to reflect any comments, perhaps by ensuring that you are applying higher-level thinking skills (Table 1.1) or have committed relevant facts to memory (**Ch 12**).

● Information retrieval and delivery

The important part of this phase will occur within the exam hall as you answer the specific questions that have been set, but it is vital to recognise that you can practise the skills involved. By doing so, you can reduce nerves and enter the exam hall with confidence. Ways of doing this are considered throughout this book, and include:

- refining the techniques you employ for memorising (**Ch 11** and **Ch 12**);
- testing yourself on individual elements you feel you need to know (**Ch 12**);
- practising answering exam questions in mock exams (**Ch 9**);
- discussing how you would approach exams and potential exam questions with a 'study buddy' (**Ch 6**);
- in quantitative subjects, practising numerical problems (**Ch 18**).

Having an exam strategy (**Ch 15**) is essential to ensure that you balance your efforts when 'delivering' information in your answers.

Practical tips for making the most of your revision time

Plan your time. Recognise that you will need to allocate time to study 'out of hours', that is, in the evenings and over weekends – at least in the short term.

Create a revision timetable. The two most important things you can do to make the most of your revision time are to create a plan for your work quickly and to stick to it in a disciplined way (**Ch 7** and **Ch 8**). Without this underpinning, all the other tips given in this book will be reduced in their effectiveness. Remember that you do not need to make your timetable into a work of art as there is always a danger that this becomes a displacement activity that prevents you getting down to real work – a common but flawed strategy that achieves a lot on paper but not much in terms of learning.

Map out the gathering, processing and retrieval aspects of revision within your revision timetable. You should set aside time for each activity.

- Information gathering must occur at the start (or should already have been accomplished), but should not take too long.
- Information processing will probably be the longest phase, and it is worth punctuating it with sessions where you deliberately cross-reference your efforts to learning objectives and past exam papers.
- Allocate some time close to the exams for practising your information retrieval skills.

Spend some time reflecting on past exam performances. Think about changes that you could make to your revision approach that might improve your future performance.

Sort out your non-academic life. You will need space and time to revise properly. Adjust your social commitments as appropriate; ask friends and family to help you out temporarily, perhaps with shopping, cooking or washing. Tidy up your working space so you can study in an organised way.

 **And now . . .**

1.1 Find out where learning objectives and past papers are located. Obtain copies at an early stage, and read them as the course material is presented, making notes about how you might wish to adjust your revision strategy to take account of them. For example, you might feel you will need to delve more deeply into certain areas, making extra notes. Alternatively, you might see that there is an expectation for you to read about a specific topic by yourself.

1.2 Create a suitable filing system. If you can develop this as your course proceeds, rather than during your revision time, you will be able to spend less time organising your notes prior to the information processing stage, and will therefore be able to spend as much time as possible understanding and learning the material.

1.3 Take the time to look into your learning personality. Consult **Ch 4** for further information. If you already have a good feel for what your learning personality is, then consider what changes to your previous revision approach you could make to take account of this.

Spoken presentations

How to give a talk or seminar with confidence

Giving a presentation can be a rewarding experience. By following simple guidelines, you can prepare yourself well, gain in confidence and communicate your message effectively.

Key topics:
→ Planning and preparing your script
→ Effective speaking
→ Using presentation software such as PowerPoint
→ Answering questions

Key terms
AV aids   Diction   Overhead transparency   PowerPoint   Prompt
Rhetorical question   Seminar

You may be expected to give a spoken presentation in several different situations – from a brief oral summary at a tutorial to a lengthy seminar on a final-year project. Your talk may be relatively casual or it may be supported by high-tech visual aids. This chapter will focus on more formal types of presentation, although similar principles apply elsewhere.

→ Planning and preparing your script

Whatever the occasion, it is important to be well prepared. Having a well-thought-out plan, good supporting material and a clear picture of your main conclusions will boost your confidence and improve your audience's experience. However, over-rehearsal can lead to a dull and monotonous delivery and you should try to avoid this.

Experienced speakers know that being slightly nervous is important, because this creates energy and sparkle when delivering the material. Their view is that if the adrenalin isn't flowing, their presentation will probably lack vitality. Turn any anxiety you may have to your advantage by thinking of it as something that will work for you rather than against you.

smart tip

Keep your introduction positive

Never start a talk by being apologetic or putting yourself down. For example, you may be tempted to say that you are unprepared or lack expertise. This will lower your audience's expectations, probably unnecessarily, and get you off to a weak start.

From Chapter 61 of *The Smarter Study Skills Companion*, 2/e. Kathleen McMillan. Jonathan Weyers. © Pearson Education Limited 2006, 2009. All rights reserved.

Start your presentation with the basics

Don't forget to begin with the seemingly obvious, such as definitions of key terms. Not all your audience may have the same background in the subject as you. If they aren't on the same wavelength, or don't understand key terms, you may lose them at the very beginning.

Structure

Every substantive presentation should have a beginning, a middle and an end. The old maxim 'say what you are going to say, say it, and then say what you have said' conforms directly to this structure and you need search no further for an outline plan.

- **Introduction.** Your task here is to introduce yourself, state the aim of your presentation, say how you intend to approach the topic and provide relevant background information.

- **Main content.** This will depend on the nature of the talk. For a talk about a project in the Sciences or Engineering, you might start with methods, and then move on to results, perhaps displayed as a series of graphs that you will lead your audience through. For a seminar in the Arts, you might discuss various aspects of your topic, giving examples or quotes as you go.

- **Conclusions.** Here your aim is to draw the talk together, explaining how all your points fit together and giving ideas of where things might develop in the future – for example, suggestions for further research or different angles to approach the subject. Finally, you should recap your whole talk in a series of 'take-home statements' and then thank your audience for their attention.

Aspects to consider when preparing a talk – a checklist

- ❏ **Audience.** Will they be experts, peers, lay people or a mixture?
- ❏ **Arrangements.** What is the date, start time and period allocated for your talk?
- ❏ **Venue.** How might the location and nature of its layout affect your delivery?
- ❏ **Facilities.** What equipment and AV aids are available?
- ❏ **Context.** Who will be preceding or following you? What introduction to you and your topic might be given?
- ❏ **Presentation style.** Do you want to use 'chalk and talk', overhead transparencies or PowerPoint?
- ❏ **Delivery.** Will you use a detailed script, prompts or simply improvise?
- ❏ **Requirements.** What might you need to bring? What equipment might you need to practise with?
- ❏ **Liaison.** Who should you contact to confirm details or make special requests?

Creating a script or series of prompts

Presentations begin as pieces of writing that evolve through several stages:

1 Creating a brainstorm or concept map of what you need to cover.

2 Laying out themes or headings with brief explanatory notes.

3 Producing a script - more or less the full text of your talk with stage directions and an indication of timing.

4 Reducing the script to a set of key words and bullet points - your prompts.

As you become more experienced, you will find you can move directly from stage 2 to stage 4, perhaps thinking through appropriate phrasing in your head rather than writing the exact words down.

Working from prompts, sometimes called 'cues', is recommended, whether they are produced as headings on cards or as bullet points in a PowerPoint slideshow (or similar). These basic headings provide the structure of your talk, so that you don't ramble or lose your place. They also help to promote an air of informality that will draw in your audience. All you need to remember is roughly what you intend to say around each point.

Reading your talk from a written script is probably a bad idea, even though you may feel more confident if you know in advance every word you are going to say. This kind of delivery always seems dry; not only because it results in an unnatural way of speaking, but also because you will be so busy looking at your script that you will almost certainly fail to make eye contact with your audience.

For similar reasons, you should probably not memorise your presentation, as this will take a lot of effort and may result in the same flat or stilted delivery, as if you had scripted it word for word. There is a happy medium where a presentation has been practised enough for the speaker to be confident, yet still convey an air of spontaneity.

- Practice will help you become more confident in the material.
- You can identify any complex parts that you cannot easily put into words, and practise these independently.
- You can find out whether your presentation will fit the allotted time.
- Make the presentation to a friend. Ask them to comment on your audibility and clarity, presentation style (including gestures) and use of visual aids.

→ Effective speaking

This is more than speaking loudly enough to be heard and pronouncing your words clearly so that the audience can make them out. These skills are fundamental - although you will already realise that many speakers fail even at this hurdle. Ask a friend to check and comment on your diction to make sure you meet these basic criteria.

Good speaking not only ensures that information is transmitted, but also engages the audience. You can do this in two main ways - through your actions and body language, and through the approach you take.

Developing your own speaking style

Every speaker has their own idiosyncrasies but some elements of style can be learned. Consider the different ways your lecturers present their material. Some will be good and some not so good (see Table 17.1). Adopt techniques you admire and try to work these into your personal style.

First, don't just stand still and speak robotically. Aim for an element of variety to keep interest levels high:

- Move around a little – but make sure you face the audience so that you will be heard, and do not pace up and down excessively.
- Use moderate hand gestures to emphasise your points – but don't wave your hands around like a windmill.
- Ensure you make eye contact with the audience – but don't stare at one person or area all the time.
- Liven your talk by shifting between modes of presentation, for example, by drawing a diagram on the board or presenting a visual aid – but don't overdo this or the audience may be distracted from your theme.

Second, try to involve your audience. Use rhetorical questions to make them think, even though you will be supplying the answers. Ask them direct questions, such as 'How many of you have read this article?' then follow up with '. . . for the benefit of those who haven't, I'll just recap on the main points'. If it would be relevant, ask them to do an activity as part of the presentation. This takes confidence to handle, but it can work well and is especially valuable to break up a longer talk where attention may wander.

Pace your talk

When you practise your talk, watch the clock and note down timing points during it. When it comes to the real thing, check how you are doing and speed up or slow down as necessary. In some cases, the real talk will take longer than you anticipated. This will either be because the initial business of getting set up has eaten up some of your allotted time, or because you have relaxed during the presentation and said more than you thought you would. In other cases, you may find that slight nervousness means you have spoken faster than intended.

→ Using presentation software such as PowerPoint

The standard methods of supporting a presentation with images and information used to be either overhead slides or 35 mm photographic slides. Overhead transparencies have the advantage over 'chalk and talk' of letting you see the same thing as your audience, while still facing them, but if filled with text they can seem dull. Slides are valuable where ultra-high-quality images are required, but an important disadvantage is that they require complex equipment and procedures to produce.

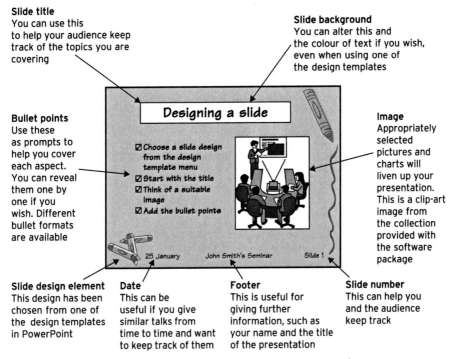

Slide title
You can use this to help your audience keep track of the topics you are covering

Slide background
You can alter this and the colour of text if you wish, even when using one of the design templates

Bullet points
Use these as prompts to help you cover each aspect. You can reveal them one by one if you wish. Different bullet formats are available

Image
Appropriately selected pictures and charts will liven up your presentation. This is a clip-art image from the collection provided with the software package

Designing a slide

☑ Choose a slide design from the design template menu
☑ Start with the title
☑ Think of a suitable image
☑ Add the bullet points

25 January   John Smith's Seminar   Slide 1

Slide design element
This design has been chosen from one of the design templates in PowerPoint

Date
This can be useful if you give similar talks from time to time and want to keep track of them

Footer
This is useful for giving further information, such as your name and the title of the presentation

Slide number
This can help you and the audience keep track

Figure 61.1 **Elements of a typical PowerPoint slide.** Similar features are available using other software.

Nowadays, both these media have largely been replaced with virtual 'slides' produced via software such as Microsoft PowerPoint. These systems provide flexibility and allow you to incorporate digital images with ease. A significant disadvantage is that a computer and (expensive) digital projector is required to show them. If you are planning to use this type of software, check whether appropriate facilities will be available in the room or can be borrowed or booked.

You can select from a variety of designs for each PowerPoint slide, most of which help you to structure your talk around a series of bullet points and to mix text with images or graphs (see Figure 61.1). This may help you to organise your prompts, but you should make sure you don't simply read them word for word from the slide. Few things are more boring than a speaker reading out what you can already see on a screen.

smart tip

Use PowerPoint to create professional overheads

If you wish to use overhead transparencies, it might be a good idea to create them first as PowerPoint slides. These can be printed as 'Slides' then copied on to special photocopy acetates or printed directly on to special material. They will be much neater and more legible than handwritten overheads. If you intend to incorporate coloured text, backgrounds or images, run tests first, however, as the projected results can be disappointing.

If you doubt your ability to speak freely around the bullet points, you can use the notes facility within PowerPoint to write down information you might not remember. You can then print out each slide and associated notes together on a single A4 page to act as a support during the presentation. Use the 'Print > Print What: > Notes Pages' command, but select 'Pure Black and White' under 'Color/grayscale' or your printout (including slide backgrounds) may appear in colour, wasting precious printer ink.

A step-by-step tutorial for setting up a PowerPoint presentation is beyond the scope of this book, but once the basics have been learned, for instance, from a handbook or online self-help tutorial, the tips shown in Table 61.1 may be useful. Always check that your version of PowerPoint is compatible with the computer system you will be using for the presentation.

Allow plenty of time for preparing presentation slides

The technology is helpful but, especially with complex material, each slide can take a lot of effort to set up. However, because of the flexibility of this system, you can save some time by merging the planning and writing phases of your talk into one session. For instance, once PowerPoint slides are constructed it is relatively easy to change their order or to alter formatting through the 'View > Master > Slide Master' function.

→ Answering questions

This is a part of a talk that many people worry about, as they have no control over what may be asked, and feel they might look stupid if they don't know an answer. Tips for dealing with this element include:

- **Prepare for likely questions.** Try to anticipate what people might ask and have an answer ready.

- **Ask for clarification if you don't understand a question fully.** You could also ask the questioner or chair to repeat the question if a part of it was indistinct or didn't seem to make sense to you.

- **Repeat the question for the benefit of those who might not have heard it.** The questioner will be facing you, not the audience, and their voice may be indistinct. This will also buy you some time for composing an answer.

- **Think before you answer.** Rather than blurting out the first thing that comes to mind, take time to weigh up the different aspects. You may feel the necessary pause is long, but this will not be how the audience perceives it.

- **If you don't know an answer, say so.** Everyone will see through a speaker who is waffling. Try saying 'I don't know the answer at the moment, but I'll find out and get back to you' if you want to say something rather than leaving a pause.

Table 61.1 Tips for constructing slides with presentation software such as PowerPoint

Aspect	Comment
Background and text colouring	Choose a background or slide design template with care. A lighter background with dark text will attract attention, but may be hard to concentrate on over the long term, whereas a darker background with light writing may be more restful on the eye.
Slide design	The standard PowerPoint designs are tried and tested, and are especially useful if you have little time to prepare for a talk, but many of your audience will have seen them before. You can easily be more original, for instance, by incorporating an image into the background, but be aware that this will take time to set up.
Text size and font	The standard PowerPoint text size defaults to values that mean that it is difficult to get much information on each slide. You can override this feature, but there is a good reason for it: cramming too much on to each slide is bad practice. A point size of 28 is probably the lowest text size you should use. Sans serif fonts, such as Arial, are said to be easiest to read on-screen.
Use of images	If you can, try to include an image in at least half of your slides. Even if these are only partially relevant, they help to maintain audience interest. A text-only presentation consisting of nothing more than bullet points will seem very dry. Use clip-art or images from copyright-free web resources if you don't have any images of your own.
Revealing your points one by one	Use the 'animation' feature to build up your slide line by line as you wish. This will help you pace your talk and ensure that the audience is listening to you, rather than reading ahead on the slide. To keep the audience on track, you may find it advantageous to use a slide giving sub-headings and reintroduce this as you move on to each new sub-topic on your list.
Use of special features	You can use special features for introducing each new slide and, within each slide, you can make text enter from different directions in different ways and even accompanied with noises. You can also link to websites (if your computer is appropriately connected) and run digital video clips. Resist the temptation to go overboard with these 'bells and whistles', because although such features can make a talk livelier, they tend to distract from your main message.
Handouts	Think about providing your audience with a handout of the slides. In PowerPoint you can use the 'File > Print > Print What: > Handouts > 6 slides per page' option to do this. When printing, it is best to select 'Pure Black and White' from the 'Color/grayscale' options, or all of the slides may print in colour, including the background. Numbering your slides (see Figure 61.1) will help your audience keep track with the handout.

 Practical tips for delivering a presentation

Dress appropriately for the occasion. You should look smart, but should feel comfortable in what you wear. Turning up in informal clothes may be interpreted as showing a lack of respect to your audience and may lead to the expectation of a sloppy presentation.

To reduce tension, take deep breaths. This can be done both before you address the audience and during pauses in your presentation.

Make sure you can be heard. At the start of your talk, ask the audience if they can hear at the back. Alternatively, when practising, try to use the room where the presentation will take place and ask a friend if they can hear you. If you know someone in the audience, you could ask them to signal to you if you are talking too quietly (or too loudly).

Make sure your audio-visual aids can be seen. If you are using some kind of projection system, make sure that you - or your shadow - don't block out the projected image. It's a good idea to ask your audience if they can see clearly before you start.

Engage the audience. Speak directly to them, not to the floor, your notes, the screen or a distant wall. Look at their faces and take cues from their reactions. If they don't seem to understand what you've said, repeat it in a different way. If they look bored, speed up, or ask a rhetorical question to engage their thoughts. Imagine the audience are your friends - speak to them with enthusiasm, warmth and genuine feeling. They will respond in kind.

Don't speak too quickly. This is a common response to nerves. Make a determined effort to slow yourself down and speak clearly.

Have a 'plan B' if your talk overruns or the projection system fails. Plan things so that you can miss something out from the main section of the talk if you are under time pressure (for example, by skipping over a few PowerPoint slides). This is preferable to being unable to complete your conclusions - people may be more interested in those than in the detail of your presentation, and they can always ask about the skipped material at the end. Print out the PowerPoint slides, perhaps in handout or note form, so that you can still use these if the projection system fails.

Try to enjoy the occasion. If you seem to be taking pleasure from speaking, your audience will also enjoy the session. Conversely, if you don't seem to be interested, why should they be?

 And now . . .

61.1 **Learn how to use presentational software in advance.** Even if you have no talk to give in the near future, time spent learning how to use PowerPoint or similar software will make it much easier, should you choose to use this form of visual aid.

61.2 **If you feel shy, take small opportunities to practise speaking so that you can build up confidence.** These might include making a comment at a meeting or asking questions at other talks - anything that gets you used to hearing your own voice speaking in a formal situation.

61.3 **Learn from other speakers.** Starting with your lecturers, think about what makes the good ones good and the bad ones bad (see also Table 17.1 on pages 116-17). Try to model your own style and presentation technique on someone whose approach you admire.

Academic writing style

How to adopt the appropriate language conventions

The stylistic codes you need to follow in academic writing are rarely comprehensively defined. This chapter will help you understand what it means to write in an academic style and outlines some forms of language to avoid.

Key topics

- What is academic style?
- Being objective
- Appropriate use of tense
- Appropriate use of vocabulary
- Appropriate use of punctuation
- Transforming non-academic to academic language

Key terms
Acronym   Colloquial   Idiom   Noun   Phrasal verb   Pronoun   Register   Rhetorical question   Verb

The format, the content and the presentation of projects and dissertations differ according to discipline. One thing that is common to all these types of writing is that they need to follow academic style. While it is possible to identify differences between 'scientific' and 'humanities' styles in the finer detail, this chapter covers the common features of all types of academic writing.

● What is academic style?

Academic style involves the use of precise and objective language to express ideas. It must be grammatically correct, and is more formal than the style used in novels, newspapers, informal correspondence and everyday conversation. This should mean that the language is clear

From Chapter 22 of *How to Write Dissertations & Project Reports*, 2/e. Kathleen McMillan & Jonathan Weyers. © Pearson Education Limited 2008, 2010, 2011. All rights reserved.

and simple. It does not imply that it is complex, pompous and dry. Above all, academic style is *objective*, using language techniques that generally maintain an impersonal tone and a vocabulary that is more succinct, rather than involving personal, colloquial, or idiomatic expressions.

British English (BE) versus American English (AE)

Academic writing in the UK nearly always adopts BE. The differences are most evident in spelling; for example, 'colour' (BE) and 'color' (AE). However, there are also differences in vocabulary, so that in AE people talk of 'professor' for 'lecturer'; and in language use, so that in AE someone might write 'we have gotten results', rather than 'we have obtained results'. In some disciplines, there is an attempt at standardisation, for example, in chemistry the spelling of 'sulphur' (BE) has become 'sulfur' (AE) as the international standard.

● Being objective

In academic writing, it is important that your personal involvement with your topic does not overshadow the importance of what you are commenting on or reporting. Generally, the main way of demonstrating this objectivity and lack of bias is by using impersonal language. This means:

● Avoiding personal pronouns – try not to use the following words:

I/me/one

you (singular and plural)

we/us.

● Using the passive rather than active voice – try to write about the action and not about the actor (the person who performed the action).

You can use other strategies to maintain an impersonal style in your writing. For general statements, you could use a structure such as 'It is . . .', 'There is . . .' or 'There are . . .' to introduce sentences. For more specific points relating to statements you have already made, you could use the structures 'This is . . .' or 'These are . . .', with appropriate tense changes according to the context. Don't forget that when you use words like 'it', 'this' or 'these', there should be no ambiguity over the word or phrase to which they refer. Clarity can be achieved by introducing a defining word (noun), for example, 'This explanation' or 'These results'.

Another way in which you can maintain objectivity by writing impersonally is to change the verb in the sentence to a noun and then reframe the sentence in a less personal way, for example:

> We **applied** pressure to the wound to stem bleeding (*verb in bold*).
> The **application** of pressure stemmed bleeding (*noun in bold*).

This kind of text-juggling will become second nature as you tackle more and more assignments.

Passive and active voice

This is best explained from examples:

- Pressure was applied to the wound to stem bleeding (passive).
- We applied pressure to the wound to stem bleeding (active).

Some would argue that the second example is clearer, but their opponents would counter-argue that the use of 'we' takes attention away from the action.

You may find that the grammar checkers in some word-processing packages suggest that passive expressions should be changed to active. However, if you follow this guidance, you will find yourself having to use a personal pronoun, which is inconsistent with impersonal academic style. If in doubt, ask your tutors for their preference.

● Appropriate use of tense

The past tense is used in academic writing to describe or comment on things that have already happened. However, there are times when the present tense is appropriate. For example, in a report you might write 'Figure 5 shows . . .', rather than 'Figure 5 showed . . .', when describing your results. A Material and Methods section, on the other hand, will always be in the past tense, because it describes what you *did*.

In colloquial English, there is often a tendency to misuse tenses. This can creep into academic writing, especially where the author is narrating a sequence of events. This can be seen by contrasting:

> Napoleon **orders** his troops to advance on Moscow. The severe winter **closes** in on them and they **come back** a ragbag of an army. (Present tense in bold.)

and:

> Napoleon **ordered** his troops to advance on Moscow. The severe winter **closed** in on them and they **came back** a ragbag of an army. (Simple past tense in bold.)

While the first of these examples might work with the soundtrack of a documentary on Napoleon's Russian campaign, it is too colloquial for academic written formats.

 Plain English

There has been a growing movement in recent times that advocates the use of 'Plain English', and it has been very successful in persuading government departments and large commercial organisations to simplify written material for public reference. This has been achieved by introducing a less formal style of language that uses simpler, more active sentence structures, and a simpler range of vocabulary avoiding jargon. This is an admirable development. However, academic writing style needs to be precise, professional and unambiguous, and the strategies of 'Plain English' campaigners may not be entirely appropriate to the style expected of you as an academic author. For the same reasons, some of the suggestions offered by software packages may be inappropriate to your subject and academic conventions.

● Appropriate use of vocabulary

Good academic writers think carefully about their choice of words. The 'Plain English' movement (see above) recommends that words of Latin origin should be replaced by their Anglo-Saxon, or spoken, alternatives. However, this does not always contribute to the style and precision appropriate to academic authorship. For example, compare:

> If we **turn down** the volume, then there will be no feedback.

and

> If we **turn down** the offer from the World Bank, then interest rates will rise.

Both sentences are meaningful, but they use the two-word verb 'turn down' in different senses. These verbs are properly called phrasal verbs and they often have more than a single meaning. Furthermore, they are also used more in speech than in formal writing. Therefore, it would be better to write:

If we *reduce* the volume, then there will be no feedback.

and

If we *reject* the offer from the World Bank, then interest rates will rise.

By using 'reduce' and 'reject' the respective meanings are clear, concise and unambiguous. If you are restricted to a word limit on your work, using the one-word verb has additional obvious advantages.

● Appropriate use of punctuation

In formal academic writing good punctuation is vital to convey meaning. However, punctuation standards are being eroded as corporate logos and design practice seek to attract the eye with unconventional print forms that ignore the correct use of capitals, apostrophes, commas and other punctuation marks. Consider the following:

1. visitors car park   (meaningless – simply a list of words)

2. Visitor's car park   (car park for a single visitor)

3. Visitors' car park   (car park for more than one visitor)

4. Visitor's car, park!   (instructing a single visitor to park)

5. Visitors, Car Park   (greeting many visitors and, rather oddly, inviting them to park or it could be a sign (a) giving directions for visitors to follow and (b) directions to a car park)

Either versions 2 or 3 could be valid and the remainder are likely to be nonsensical. This example serves to demonstrates how clear punctuation avoids ambiguity. Without punctuation or with inappropriate punctuation, sentences become meaningless or, worse still, confusing and/or impenetrable. Table 22.1 illustrates some of the more common errors that appear regularly in student writing, models the correction and explains the error.

139

Table 22.1 **Common punctuation errors and their corrections.** The following common errors with their corrections should help you to find an answer to most punctuation dilemmas.

Punctuation mark	Error	Correction	Explanation
1.1 Apostrophes: singular	The **Principals'** Committee will meet at noon today.	Principal's	There is only one Principal, therefore the apostrophe goes immediately after the word 'Principal'. Then add the 's' to make it correctly possessive.
1.2 Apostrophes: plural	The **womens'** team beat the **mens'** team by 15 points and the **childrens'** team beat them both. The **boy's** team won the prize.	women's men's children's boys'	The words 'women', 'men' and 'children' are plural words. To make them possessive, just add an apostrophe after the plural word and add 's'. The word 'boys' is a plural and is a regularly formed plural, thus, the apostrophe comes after the 's'.
1.3 Apostrophes: contractions	**Its** not a good time to sell a property. **Its** been up for sale for ages. **Well** need to lower the price.	It's = it is It's = it has We'll = we shall	'It's' is a contracted form of the words 'It is' or 'it has'. In this case, the sentence means: 'It is not a good time to sell a property'.
1.4 Apostrophes: not needed	The **tomatoes'** cost 60 pence a kilo.	tomatoes	The word 'tomatoes' is a plural. No apostrophe is needed to make words plural.
1.5 Apostrophes: not needed	The Charter includes human rights in **it's** terms.	its	No apostrophe needed to show possession.
2.1 Capital letters: sentences	**the** first day of the term is tomorrow.	The	The first letter of the first word of a sentence in English always needs a capital letter.
2.2 Capital letters: proper names	The **prime minister** is the first **lord of the treasury.** The **north atlantic treaty organisation** is a regional organisation. Pearls found in the **river tay** are of considerable value.	Prime Minister; First Lord of the Treasury North Atlantic Treaty Organisation River Tay	Proper nouns for roles, names of organisations, rivers, mountains, lochs, lakes and place names. These all require a capital for all parts of the name.

3 Colon	A number of aspects will be covered, including • Energy conservation • Pollution limitation • Cost control	... including: • energy conservation; • pollution limitation; • cost control.	A colon to introduce the list. Each item, except the last one, should be finished with a semi-colon. No capital is necessary at each bullet if the list follows from an incomplete sentence introducing the list.
4.1 Commas	**The leader of the group Dr Joan Jones** was not available for comment.	The leader of the group, Dr Joan Jones, was not available for comment.	This is a common error. The name of the person gives more information about the leader; thus, the person's name needs to be inserted with commas before and after.
4.2 Commas	There are several member-states that do not support this view. They are **Britain France Germany Portugal and Greece.**	There are several member-states that do not support this view. They are Britain, France, Germany, Portugal, and Greece.	Strictly speaking, when making a list such as in the example, a comma should come before 'and'. This is called the 'Oxford comma' and its use has caused much debate. However, increasingly, the comma is being omitted before the word 'and' in lists such as this one.
4.3 Commas	**However** we have no evidence to support this statement.	However, we have no evidence to support this statement.	The 'signposting' words often used at the beginning of sentences are followed by a comma. Some of the more common of these words are: however, therefore, thus, hence, nevertheless, moreover, in addition.
4.4 Commas	**Although we have had significant rainfall** the reservoirs are low.	Although we have had significant rainfall, the reservoirs are low.	When a sentence begins with 'although', then the sentence has two parts. The part that gives the idea of concession in this sentence is 'Although we have had significant rainfall'. The second part gives us the impact of that concession, in this case, that 'the reservoirs are low'. A comma is used to divide these parts.
4.5 Commas	**To demonstrate competence it** is important to be able to face challenges.	To demonstrate competence, it is important to be able to face challenges.	Another way to write this sentence would be: 'It is important to be able to face challenges to demonstrate competence'. By putting the phrase 'to demonstrate competence' at the beginning of the sentence, it places emphasis on the idea of competence and, in order to make that word-order distinction, a comma is needed.
5 Ellipsis	There is a deficit in the budget......brought on by mismanagement at the highest level.	There is a deficit in the budget ... brought on by mismanagement at the highest level.	Ellipsis marks always consist of three dots, no more.

● Transforming non-academic to academic language

Thinking about the style of your writing should be a feature of any review you make of drafts of your written work, Table 22.2 gives a specific example of text conversion from informal to formal style. Table 22.3 provides several pointers to help you achieve a more academic style.

Table 22.2 Example of converting a piece of 'non-academic' writing into academic style. Note that the conversion results in a slightly longer piece of text (47 versus 37 words): this emphasises the point that while you should aim for concise writing, precise wording may be more important.

Original text (non-academic style)	'Corrected' text (academic style)
In this country, we have changed the law so that the King or Queen is less powerful since the Great War. But he or she can still advise, encourage or warn the Prime Minister if they want.	In the United Kingdom, legislation has been a factor in the decline of the role of the monarchy in the period since the Great War. Nevertheless, the monarchy has survived and, thus, the monarch continues to exercise the right to advise, encourage and warn the Prime Minister.
Points needing correction	**Corrected points**
● Non-specific wording (*this country*)	● Specific wording (country specified: *in the United Kingdom*)
● Personal pronoun (*we*)	● Impersonal language (*legislation has*)
● Weak grammar (*but* is a connecting word and should not be used to start a sentence).	● Appropriate signpost word (*nevertheless*)
● Word with several meanings (*law*)	● Generic, yet well-defined term (*legislation*)
● Duplication of nouns (*king or queen*)	● Singular abstract term (*monarch*)
● Inconsistent and potentially misleading pronoun use (*he or she, they*)	● Repeated subject (*monarch*) and reconstructed sentence
● Informal style (*can still*)	● More formal style (*continues to exercise*)

Table 22.3 **Fundamentals of academic writing.** These elements of academic writing are laid out in alphabetical order. Being aware of these elements and training yourself to follow them will help you to develop as an academic author and will ensure that you don't lose marks by making some basic errors of usage or expression. This is particularly important in longer texts such as dissertations or project reports.

Abbreviations and acronyms
It is acceptable to use abbreviations in academic writing to express units, for example, SI units. Otherwise, abbreviations are generally reserved for note-taking. Thus, avoid: e.g. (for example), i.e. (that is), viz. (namely) in formal work.
Acronyms are a kind of abbreviation formed by taking the initial letters of a name of an organisation, a procedure or an apparatus, and then using these letters instead of writing out the title in full. Thus, World Health Organisation becomes WHO. The academic convention is that the first time that you use a title with an acronym alternative, then you should write it in full with the acronym in brackets immediately after the full title. Thereafter, within that document you can use the acronym. For example:
The European Free Trade Association (EFTA) has close links with the European Community (EC). Both EFTA and the EC require new members to have membership of the Council of Europe as a prerequisite for admission to their organisations.
In some forms of academic writing, for example, formal reports, you may be expected to include a list of abbreviations in addition to these first-time-of-use explanations.

'Absolute' terms
In academic writing, it is important to be cautious about using absolute terms such as:
always and **never; most** and **all; least** and **none.**
This does not prevent you from using these words; it simply means that they should be used with caution, that is, when you are absolutely certain of your ground (see p. 149).

Clichés
Living languages change and develop over time. This means that some expressions come into such frequent usage that they lose their meaning; indeed, they can often be replaced with a much less long-winded expression. For example:
First and foremost (first); **last but not least** (finally); **at this point in time** (now).
This procedure is the **gold standard** of hip replacement methods. (This procedure is the best hip replacement method.)
In the second example, 'gold standard' is completely inappropriate; correctly used, it should refer to monetary units, but it has been misused by being introduced into other contexts.

▶

Table 22.3 continued

Colloquial language
This term encompasses informal language that is common in speech. Colloquialisms and idiomatic language should not be used in academic writing. This example shows how colloquial language involving cliché and idiom has been misused: **Not to beat about the bush**, increasing income tax did the Chancellor **no good at the end of the day** and he **was ditched** at the next Cabinet reshuffle. (Increasing income tax did not help the Chancellor and he was replaced at the next Cabinet reshuffle.)

'Hedging' language
For academic purposes, it is often impossible to state categorically that something is or is not the case. There are verbs that allow you to 'hedge your bets' by not coming down on one side or another of an argument, or which allow you to present a variety of different scenarios without committing yourself to any single position, for example: **seems that   looks as if   suggests that   appears that.** This involves using a language construction that leaves the reader with the sense that the evidence presented is simply supporting a hypothetical, or imaginary, case. To emphasise this sense of 'hedging', the use of a special kind of verb is introduced. These are: **can/cannot   could/could not   may/may not   might/might not.** These can be used with a variety of other verbs to increase the sense of tentativeness. For example: These results **suggest** that there has been a decline in herring stocks in the North Sea. Even more tentatively, this could be: These results **could suggest** that there has been a decline in herring stocks in the North Sea.

Jargon and specialist terms
Most subjects make use of language in a way that is exclusive to that discipline. It is important, therefore, to explain terms that a general reader might not understand. It is always good practice to define specialist terms or 'regular' words that are being used in a very specific way.

Rhetorical questions
Some writers use direct rhetorical questions as a stylistic vehicle to introduce the topic addressed by the question. This is a good strategy if you are making a speech and it can have some power in academic writing, although it should be used sparingly. Example: **How do plants survive in dry weather?** This might be a question starting a chapter. It could be rephrased as: Understanding how plants survive in dry weather is important.

Table 22.3 continued

Split infinitives
One of the most commonly quoted split infinitives comes from the TV series *Star Trek* where Captain James T. Kirk states that the aim of the Star Ship Enterprise is 'to boldly go where no man has gone before'. This means that an adverb (boldly) has split the infinitive (to go). It should read as 'to go boldly'. Many traditionalists consider that the split infinitive is poor English, although modern usage increasingly ignores the rule. Nevertheless, it is probably better to avoid the split infinitive in academic writing, which tends to be particularly traditional.

Value judgements
These are defined as statements in which the author or speaker is providing an interpretation based on a subjective viewpoint (see p. 148). For example, a writer who states that 'Louis XIV was a rabid nationalist' without giving supporting evidence for this statement is not making an objective comment in a professional manner. Rewording this statement to: 'Louis XIV was regarded as a rabid nationalist. This is evident in the nature of his foreign policy where he . . .' offers the reader some evidence that explains the claim.

 ## Practical tips for ensuring that you write in an academic style

Think about your audience. Your readers should direct the style you adopt for any writing you do. For example, if you were writing to your bank manager asking for a loan, you would not use text-messaging or informal language. For academic writing, you should take into account that your reader(s) will probably be assessing your work and, in addition to knowledge and content, they will be looking for evidence of awareness and correct use of specialist terms and structures.

Avoid contractions. In spoken English, shortened forms such as, don't, can't, isn't, it's, I'd and we'll are used all the time. However, in academic written English, they should not be used. Texting contractions are also inappropriate.

Avoid personal pronouns. Experiment with other language structures so that you avoid the personal pronouns, *I/me/one*, *you* and *we/us*, and their possessive forms, *my*, *your* and *our*.

Take care with style in reflective writing. Some subjects, such as Nursing, Education and Social Work, involve student practitioners in a process of reflection on professional contexts and their roles within them. When this type of requirement is part of a written assessment, then moderate use of the first person (I or we) is expected. If your subject requires this approach, then balance your use of personal identification with the more neutral style expected more generally in academic circles. In other words, don't overuse the words 'I' or 'we'.

Avoid sexist language. The Council of Europe recommends that, where possible, gender-specific language be avoided. Thus: 'S/he will provide specimens for her/his exam'. This is rather clumsy, but, by transforming the sentence into the plural, this is avoided: 'They will provide specimens for their exams'. Alternatively, 'you' and 'your' could be used.

(GO) And now . . .

22.1 **Take steps to improve your grammar.** You may be able to find repeated errors that your supervisor or other lecturers have identified in your work. Highlight points that you do not know how to rectify at present and resolve to find further information. You can do this by consulting a grammar book – for example, Foley and Hall (2003) – to find out more about the relevant grammar point. You can consolidate your understanding by doing the exercises provided in such books.

22.2 **Ask a friend to work with you on your writing style.** Swap a piece of writing and check over your friend's writing and ask them to do the same for yours. When you have done this, compare the points you have found. Try to explain what you think could be improved. Together, you may be able to clarify some aspects that you were unaware were problematic. Afterwards, follow the suggestion in point 22.1 above.

22.3 **Learn from published academic writing in your discipline.** Look at a textbook or journal article – especially in the area that discusses results or evidence or recommendations. Try to find examples of the use of 'hedging' language (Table 22.3) and note what else authors do with language in order to ensure that they avoid implying absolute judgements.

Structuring your argument

Introduction

It started in your head. Then it became a jumble of notes on the page. Now you have to translate this highly personal tangle of ideas into something comprehensible to the world. You have to communicate your argument. This chapter shows how this can be done.

At this stage your argument may make perfect sense to you. It may indeed seem utterly precious and beyond all improvement. However, you still have to find a way of explaining it. You have to get it across to people who are reading at speed and who, perhaps, are tired and bored with the effort of marking dozens of scripts. In order to do this you have to learn how to read your own work. Learning how to read your own work involves seeing your efforts through the eyes of a hard-to-convince, heard-it-all-before, sceptic. This cantankerous alter ego should be leaning over your shoulder from first draft to final copy. Its presence is especially valuable as you begin to organise your argument, as you give it shape and structure.

Step 1: Sketching it out

In the course of any normal day I find myself involved in a number of arguments. They may take the form of a chat with a friend or shouting at a kitchen utensil (or vice versa). As ordinary, day-to-day events these encounters work fine. Spontaneous, off-the-cuff, and without forethought, they suit their context perfectly well. Academic arguments can't be like that. More to the point, they don't need to be like that because they are **prepared**. If you are given the opportunity to work out an argument, if you have hours, days or weeks to structure it, then it must appear carefully considered and organised.

From Chapter 2 of *How to argue, Essential skills for writing and speaking convincingly*, 2/e. Alastair Bonnett. © Alastair Bonnett 2008. All rights reserved.

Students are constantly told to plan their essays, to sketch them out. Without any assistance to develop an intellectual project this mantra can easily appear not only tedious but an attempt to straitjacket the imagination. However, when it is used to enable your intellectual ambitions such advice becomes something liberatory, an essential tool to enable you to get your message, your point of view, across.

Webs and arrows

As the phrase 'sketching an argument' implies, the first stage in communicating your ideas to a wider audience is a graphic one. Literally drawing your argument, representing it through webs, arrows, boxes and so on, is essential because simplification is essential. Picturing your argument demands that you break your ideas down into easily understood and separate parts. It demands that you show the connections between these parts in a straightforward, easy-to-grasp, fashion. This act of simplification may sometimes seem to do terrible violence to the baroque details of your original argument. But that is the price of communication. Coherence before complexity.

Everyone has their own style for sketching out an argument. The two most popular methods are **spider diagrams** and **flow diagrams**. Children are often introduced to spider diagrams in school. But whatever your age they are an effective way of generating ideas and seeing the links between them. Spider diagrams start with the question or topic you are going to explore. This goes at the centre of the web. From this point ideas thread outwards, creating a (usually rather lop-sided) web or tree-like structure. Spider diagrams are excellent for the initial, creative, stage of your argument. They are not so good in helping you turn all those ideas into a coherent and plausible essay. When written up, the messy fun of the spider's web can collapse into a jumble of unconnected paragraphs. Thus I would recommend that, having done your spider diagram, you move on to something more formal. A structured, flow diagram method is introduced below. It has four stages.

1 Identify the different parts of your argument

Each of these parts represents a key section of your argument. Identify as few of these as you can get away with. Where appropriate, you may wish to treat these parts as indicating the potential subtitles of your essay. At this stage don't order the parts in any sequence but do give them titles. Again, these titles should be as simple as possible. The example I shall use takes the form of an argument against another author (called Brown). My illustration uses only four basic elements: 'Introduction', 'Counter-evidence', 'Brown's thesis' and 'Conclusion'.

2 Arrange the parts in logical sequence, drawing an arrow between them

The sequence of some of your parts (the introduction, for example) will be obvious. However, you may need to play around with the ordering of the others, testing out whether one really does usefully build on and logically proceed from the other. The most important rule here is a negative one: if part *y* requires part *x* to make any sense, then *x* has to go before *y*. Generally, arguments should be cumulative, their elements should appear to arise from work already introduced. This isn't an iron rule (and some confident arguers like to flout it) but it is good advice.

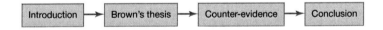

3 Unpack the contents of each part

Each of the parts of your essay is like a mini-essay. They should have beginnings, middles and endings. At this stage it is usually appropriate to introduce other key references, theories and positions attached to a name or label that your argument is going to engage (in the illustration, I've chosen to engage two named authors, Blue and Green). Some people prefer to unpack each part into a sequence of mini-parts, a procedure that makes sure you attend to the logical flow of each section. However, at this micro level, webs can be just as good. Moreover, webs have the advantage of expressing the complexity of linkages (i.e. the way the different parts of your essay connect) and of being more open to creative thought.

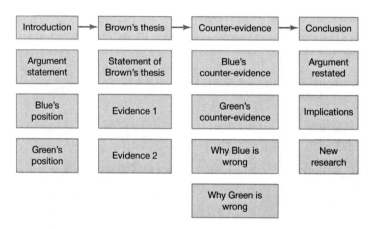

4 Draw secondary arrows showing connections between the different parts of your argument

The last phase in sketching your argument is about locating those key links between different parts of your argument that do not appear in the earlier models. You should be making sure that claims made in the introduction are taken up elsewhere and that important new connections that have suddenly struck you are attended to. Now is also a good moment to deal with potential criticism. It is often during this final phase that writers make sure that they have 'dealt with' potential counter-arguments. Ask yourself, 'What other material or causes could be claimed as relevant here?' and 'What objections could be made to this argument?' If you find that these questions make your argument appear untenable then you must abandon it or radically redesign it.

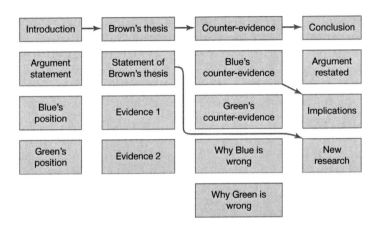

Step 1: Summary

Identify the different stages of your argument. Sketch them out in sequence, showing the connections between and within each stage.

Keep your sketch as simple as possible.

Step 2: The one-sentence summary (smooth version)

As you move closer to formally presenting your argument you need to start formulating the particular words and phrases that can communicate your central point. You need to deliver your argument in a way that renders it immediately graspable, in a way that allows readers no excuse for misunderstanding you. At this stage roughly written and personal summaries no longer suffice. In the light of your sketched-out structure you should be able to produce a version of your argument that is coherent, clear and grammatical.

If your essay is not going to be purely theoretical then you will need to include in your one-sentence summary a reference to the empirical evidence you will be drawing on to establish your case.

At this stage the so-called **one-sentence summary** can actually be two or even three lines long if necessary. While you don't want a summary that looks like a paragraph, you do want to avoid collapsing your argument into something simplistic. The key is to make your summary as short as your argument will allow. A lot rests on this concise summary. It will be your 'hook line', something that withstands repetition and to which readers or listeners can easily respond. It is certainly worth taking time with its composition and experimenting with different versions.

Step 2: Summary

Write a concise summary of your argument. Don't rush it. This is your 'hook-line'.

Step 3: Putting it all together

If you have completed all the steps outlined so far in this book then actually delivering your argument will be relatively straightforward. You have done the bulk of the intellectual work, you have sorted out your structure and you have encapsulated your core thesis in summary form. All you need to do now is put all this together. In this section I will outline five key things that students should always consider when composing their argument.

fit

If you are writing your essay, rather than presenting it orally, you have the considerable luxury of being able to rework your argument as you deliver it. However, if it is basically sound, I'd advise against adding much supplementary material at this stage. If you have a coherent and interesting line to take then trying to stuff in a load more theses, hypotheses and so on is going to wreck your essay. As Chapter 1 explained, good arguments have a clear and precise focus. To jeopardise that focus is to take a great risk.

Finally, don't forget that arguments arise as a consequence of engaging with debate. This means that references to your source materials need to be woven into your text in the first draft. Sources are not incidentals that can be tacked on at the end. You are writing within a community of scholars. The more clearly you communicate and acknowledge this fact the more informed and sophisticated your work will be judged to be.

The introduction: the most important part of your essay

State your argument clearly and early

The introduction matters. It matters because on any large course (i.e. of over 30 students) you need to make an early impact if your composition is to have a chance of being noticed. It also matters because it is the introduction that establishes your argument. You cannot leave it until the end, nor can you wait for it to dawn on the marker on page 26. You need to get your argument in early (this is true whether your assignment is 20,000 or 500 words). In crude terms, all the material you write after you state your argument is working for you; all the material you write before it is merely preamble.

My personal ideal is for preambles, introductory context and so on not to be longer than one or two paragraphs. The argument should then be stated as a one-sentence summary. And it should be formulated *explicitly* as an argument. Don't allow your readers to miss it. Write something such as 'In this essay it will be argued …'. Remember, where appropriate your summary argument should make reference to the empirical material that you are going to be drawing on.

Make it clear that you are going to engage in debate

The introduction should also be used to tell the reader that your essay is going to engage in debate. In other words you need to indicate that you know an academic literature exists on the subjects you will be addressing and that you are going to 'take sides' or take issue with positions expressed in this debate. Using references, naming authors and/or key texts, and doing so early on in your essay, is nearly always good practice.

State your structure

After stating your argument and indicating the nature of the debate you are engaging, it is usually appropriate to explain the structure of your contribution. This applies to short projects and oral deliveries just as much as it does to long essays. Readers and listeners like to know where they are going. Academic essays are not about the thrill of surprise. Your introduction needs to communicate exactly what is going to be said and how it is going to be evidenced. Being explicit about what you are doing provides less excuse for your markers to write 'poor structure' or 'no clear argument' on their appraisal sheets. It's not imaginative or very sparkling but something like this will do the job for you: 'This essay has three sections. In section one … In section two … Finally, in section three …'.

How to use empirical material

Some students find that once they have mastered argument another problem surfaces. Where once their essays were dominated by 'mere description' now they appear in danger of consisting of 'mere argument'. In other words they feel they don't know how to handle 'evidence', how to 'work it in' to their analysis. This problem is apparent in essays that switch suddenly and awkwardly back and forth from theory to observation, moving clumsily from clearly expressed argument to subsections composed of a jumble of data.

Arguments do not consist simply of introductions and conclusions. They exist to make sense of your facts, to interpret your data. As this implies, your empirical material must be fully introduced at the time you state your argument, i.e. in the introduction. It also means that you need to be constantly returning to the terms and content of your argument while you are considering your empirical material. Your essay is your argument; everything else makes sense because of it. If you find yourself describing things that do not serve a function within your argument and which have no role in your analysis, then you probably need to reassess your direction and start red-lining tangential information.

Although empirical tangents should be avoided it is usually appropriate to treat one's data as complex. More specifically, it is sensible to regard it as diverse and nuanced. Students often make the mistake of homogenising their empirical material, of imagining that it evidences only one point. This leads to meaningless repetition. For example, when using qualitative interview data, pages of quotes are sometimes used to prove the same point again and again. This wastes your data, is very boring to read and gives the impression that you have not 'listened' carefully to your data. After all, it is highly unlikely that such a varied source would repeatedly exemplify exactly the same idea or theme. A more probable and useful outcome is that such data would illustrate different points of emphasis, different reasons to

support your overall analysis. This observation could be extended to other kinds of material. Your argument is better served by having it confirmed from a variety of positions than from just one.

> Always relate your evidence back to your argument and avoid repetition of evidence.

How to handle theory

Theories are arguments, or, more precisely, theories are arguments recognised as significant and given a name. As this implies, engaging with theory is just another way of saying you are engaging with a known and debated argument. Theory is impossible to avoid. However this isn't the same thing as saying that you are obliged to place your work within some grand and broadly sketched theoretical context. Indeed it is usually better to be as specific as possible. If one wishes to situate one's work in relation to structuralism, for example, it is better to say what sort of structuralism and whose structuralism than to flatten out that enormously diverse tradition into a series of bland abstractions.

The secret of engaging with theory is not to be found in peppering one's text with 'ologies' and 'isms' or making general and generalising half-understood 'big ideas'. Rather it is to be found in being as precise and focused as possible. Here are some 'dos' and 'don'ts' designed to assist you in this task.

Do:

- Flag up your engagement with relevant theory in your introduction. Be particular: refer to specific theories and make reference to named proponents and/or named schools.

- Suggest that you know there are alternative paths within the theory you are engaging.

- Explain why you are using this theory.

- Get some contemporary theoretical references into your essay (to avoid giving the impression that you are 'behind the debate').

- Use short sentences. This will help keep your explanations comprehensible.

- Define your theory. It is likely to have different interpretations, so it is important to make yours clear.

Don't:

- Claim too much. It is unlikely that you can refute, or adequately engage with, all the theoretical traditions relevant to your topic. Moreover, unqualified statements such as 'This essay will prove that behaviourism is wrong', or 'This essay will take a postmodern approach' look ignorant. Far better to make more precise claims, such as 'This essay identifies a limitation with behaviourist methodology' or 'This essay applies the techniques of Derridean deconstruction'.

- Use too many theories. One or two theoretical traditions are usually enough. Dragging in more perspectives is going to confuse readers and distract from your main argument. Your essay cannot scan its topic from every angle. Rather it should be offering a specific, useful and self-consciously limited contribution.

- Adopt positions that you don't believe in. It isn't necessary.

- Refer to material that you don't understand. Sometimes you might get away with it but, sooner or later, you'll be found out. It is not a risk worth taking. If you don't understand a theory or area within a theory then avoid writing about it until such time as you do.

Returning to your argument

In the conclusion or penultimate section of your essay you will need to return explicitly to your central argument. You will also need to say how you have demonstrated and/or proven your central point. As this implies, returning to your argument is not simply a matter of repeating it. At this stage you should be able to discuss it in the light of your evidence and your analysis. It is often appropriate to use this moment to provide an **extended** account of your argument, to flesh out the one-sentence summary of the introduction into a paragraph that can reflect the subtleties of your position. Phrases such as 'This essay has demonstrated that

. . .', or 'As I have shown in this essay . . .' are handy at this point. They remind the reader that the essay has achieved something, that it has fulfilled its initial claims.

> Return to your argument towards the end, emphasising what your essay has achieved.

End with a bang, not a whimper

If you want your essay to have an impact, then your conclusion needs to grab readers' attention. Merely summarising your argument or plodding through a précis of your data is not going to do this. One useful strategy is to rephrase the essay's basic aim in much bolder language. In the conclusion it is often appropriate to articulate your objectives in a punchy, direct fashion (perhaps using personal pronouns and very short sentences). This should be combined with a much more formal explanation. Using both styles can provide a simultaneously stimulating and convincing conclusion to your essay.

Your conclusion should also be used to remind readers of the limitations of your approach. 'This essay has not attempted to ...', or 'The focus of this essay has been limited to ...' are phrases that indicate that you recognise the specificity of your argument. Conclusions can also be used to sketch out the wider implications of your position. This can be done by offering speculative arguments and by suggesting possible new areas of research. Both need to be treated seriously. You must be specific about what kinds of research you have in mind and about why they would be useful. Rather than thinking about your conclusion as a dead end you should imagine it as a room with many open doors. Good conclusions give a sense of possibilities, of the ongoing nature of debate.

> Your conclusion needs to reignite the reader's interest in your argument and the wider debate.

Step 3: Summary

Good arguments have a clear aim and structure. Your argument needs to be sustained throughout your text, both empirically and theoretically. Your conclusion should reiterate your argument and indicate its importance.

EXERCISES

Exercise 1 Practising the sketch, I

Sketching out essay plans is something that one becomes better at with practice. Trying to map out an essay on a topic that you know little about provides some of the best practice of all (because it allows you to focus on the issue of structure without being distracted by content). Below are five arguments. Your task is to sketch them out using the model presented in Step 1 (stages 1 and 2 should suffice).

- The notion of a 'Spanish literary tradition' is a nationalist myth.
- Advanced farming technology is not a sustainable resource within either the developing or developed countries.
- British and French race relations legislation is premised on different conceptions of the reality and desirability of racial demarcation.
- Surrealist novels employ the sexuality of women to represent the content and practice of primitive freedom.
- Modern physics is a product of the Enlightenment but quantum physics is not.

Exercise 2 Practising the sketch, II

This is a more testing exercise. Again you will need to produce a graphic model of an argument. However, this time there is more information to deal with and your model needs to be correspondingly more complex. You will need to employ stages 1, 2 and 3 (and perhaps 4) of the model presented in Step 1 in order to do justice to the examples.

159

You can also use these three passages to practise writing one-sentence summaries. Remember, these need to be both concise and informative.

> Modern imperialism, it is usually held, intensified the large-scale regional differentiation of the globe ... The colonialism of the Middle Ages was quite different. When Anglo-Normans settled in Ireland or Germans in Pomerania or Castilians in Andalusia, they were not engaged in the creation of a pattern of regional subordination. What they were doing was reproducing units similar to those in their homelands. The towns, churches and estates they established simply replicated the social framework they knew from back home. The net result of this colonialism was not the creation of 'colonies', in the sense of dependencies, but the spread, by a kind of cellular multiplication, of the cultural and social forms found in the Latin Christian core. The new lands were closely integrated with the old. Travellers in the later Middle Ages going from Magdeburg to Berlin and on to Wroclaw, or from Burgos to Toledo and on to Seville, would not be aware of crossing any decisive social or cultural frontier. (Robert Bartlett, *The Making of Europe: Conquest, Colonization and Cultural Change 950–1350*, 1993)

> One of the greatest enemies of science is pseudo-science. In a scientific age, prejudice and passion seek to clothe themselves in a garb of scientific respectability; and when they cannot find support from true science, they invent a pseudo-science to justify themselves. We all know that the Devil can quote Scripture for his own purpose: today we are finding that he can even invent a false Scripture from which to quote.
>
> Nowhere is this lamentable state of affairs more pronounced than in regard to 'race'. A vast pseudo-science of 'racial biology' has been erected which serves to justify political ambitions, economic ends, social grudges, class prejudices. (Julian Huxley and A. C. Haddon, *We Europeans: A Survey of 'Racial' Problems*, 1935)

Revenge is a kind of wild justice; which the more man's nature runs to, the more ought law to weed it out. For as for the first wrong, it doth but offend the law; but the revenge of that wrong, putteth the law out of office. Certainly, in taking revenge, a man is but even with his enemy; but in passing it over, he is superior: for it is a prince's part to pardon. And Solomon, I am sure, saith, It is the glory of a man to pass by an offence. That which is past, is gone, and irrevocable; and wise men have enough to do, with things present, and to come: therefore, they do but trifle with themselves, that labour in past matters. (Francis Bacon, *Essays*, 1985; originally published 1625)

Exercise 3 Evidence and argument

It is important to integrate your evidence into your argument. A useful way of thinking about this issue is to pay attention to the way people in the media, such as journalists, employ their facts. The exercise that follows is a very simple but often highly revealing way of interrogating this relationship.

First of all you need to choose a newspaper article or television presentation (the latter will need to be taped). Try and pick something that is short yet appears to be addressing substantive issues (this makes the exercise easier). The exercise has three stages:

1   Your initial act of analysis is to note down the basic, overall argument that is being put forward. As always you should try and express this in as concise yet informative terms as possible.
2   Then write down *all* the evidence that is being offered by the news source in question to support this argument, however slight.
3   The next step is to arrange this information into five columns: 'proves' (i.e. no more evidence is required), 'strongly supports' (i.e. offers substantial support but not proof of the argument), 'weakly supports' and 'irrelevant'. Where evidence is merely being repeated then it should be noted in both one of the four preceding columns and the fifth column, which can be labelled 'repeats'.

Although this exercise can be completed by one person it is also effective when conducted by a group (with all participants using the same piece of journalism). Having completed the exercise, each member of the group should then identify what they consider to be a key or illuminating piece of information from the first, second and fourth columns (i.e. 'proves', 'strongly supports' and 'irrelevant'). These items can then be compared and used as the basis of a discussion on the relationship between evidence and argument within the group. Evidence from the other columns is useful to supplement these discussions.

Thinking critically

How to develop a logical approach to analysis and problem-solving

The ability to think critically is probably the most transferable of the skills you will develop at university and is vital for completing a dissertation or project report successfully. Your future employers will expect you to be able use it to tackle professional challenges. This chapter introduces concepts, methods and fallacies to watch out for when trying to improve your analytical capabilities.

Key topics
- Thinking about thinking
- Using method to prompt and organise your thoughts
- Recognising fallacies and biased presentations

Key terms
Bias   Critical thinking   Fallacy   Propaganda   Value judgement

How can you apply theory and technique to help you think better? Many specialists believe that critical thinking is a skill that you can develop through practice. This is an assumption that lies behind much of higher education. Your experience of university probably tells you that your grades have depended increasingly on the analysis of facts and the ability to arrive at an opinion and support it with relevant information, rather than the simple recall of fact. This is especially true when the assessed outcome is a piece of critical writing like a project report or dissertation. If you understand the underlying processes a little better, this should help you meet the expectations of your supervisor(s) and examiner(s).

From Chapter 14 of *How to Write Dissertations & Project Reports*, 2/e. Kathleen McMillan & Jonathan Weyers. © Pearson Education Limited 2008, 2010, 2011. All rights reserved.

Definition: critical

People often interpret the words 'critical' and 'criticism' to mean being negative about an issue. For university work, the alternative meaning of 'making a careful judgement after balanced consideration of all aspects of a topic' is the one you should adopt.

● Thinking about thinking

Benjamin Bloom, a noted educational psychologist, and colleagues, identified six different steps involved in learning and thinking within education:

- knowledge
- comprehension
- application
- analysis
- synthesis
- evaluation.

Bloom *et al.* (1956) showed that students naturally progressed through this scale of thought-processing during their studies (Table 14.1). From this table, you may recognise that your early education mainly focussed on knowledge, comprehension and application, while learning at university requires more in terms of analysis, synthesis and evaluation.

Thus, it is important to recognise that simple description alone is not sufficient at the higher-order level of thought required in the construction of a dissertation or project report. Thinking critically means that you need to construct an analysis of different viewpoints or approaches, for example, by looking at the issue or problem from different perspectives. The matrix note-making strategy shown in Figure 10.6 shows a practical way in which to tackle this on paper. This approach can be adapted for many different sorts of analysis across a range of disciplines. By considering different positions, ideas, viewpoints or approaches, it is possible to weigh them up according to criteria that you set for yourself. In the context of the research required for dissertations or projects, these critical faculties will

Table 14.1 **Bloom *et al.*'s classification of thinking processes (Bloom *et al.* 1956) ('Bloom's taxonomy')**

Thinking processes (in ascending order of difficulty)	Typical actions
Knowledge. If you know a fact, you have it at your disposal and can *recall* or *recognise* it. This does not mean you necessarily understand it at a higher level.	• Defining • Describing • Identifying
Comprehension. To comprehend a fact means that you *understand* what it means.	• Contrasting • Discussing • Interpreting
Application. To apply a fact means that you can *put it to use.*	• Demonstrating • Calculating • Illustrating
Analysis. To analyse information means that you are able to *break it down into parts* and show how these components *fit together.*	• Analysing • Explaining • Comparing
Synthesis. To synthesise, you need to be able to *extract relevant facts* from a body of knowledge and use these to *address an issue in a novel way* or *create something new.*	• Composing • Creating • Integrating
Evaluation. If you evaluate information, you *arrive at a judgement* based on its importance relative to the topic being addressed.	• Recommending • Supporting • Drawing a conclusion

enable you to examine strong and weak dimensions, identify and construct lines of argument and support these with relevant evidence drawn from the literature. Table 14.2 provides examples of the way in which different stages of thought-processing can apply in three different disciplines.

● Using method to prompt and organise your thoughts

If you adopt a methodical approach to the analysis of problems – not only academic ones – then you will become skilled in thinking critically. The pointers below will help you arrive at a logical answer. You should regard this as a menu rather than a recipe – think about the different stages and how they might be useful for the specific research issue that you are tackling and your own style of working. Adopt or reject them as you see fit, according to your needs, and chop and change their order as appropriate.

Table 14.2 Examples of Bloom's classification of thinking processes within representative university subjects (Bloom *et al.*, 1956)

Thinking processes (in ascending order of complexity)	Examples		
	Law	Arts subjects, e.g. History or Politics	Numerical subjects
Knowledge	You might know the name and date of a case, statute or treaty without understanding its relevance	You might know that a river was an important geographical and political boundary in international relations, without being able to identify why	You might be able to write down a particular mathematical equation, without understanding what the symbols mean or where it might be applied
Comprehension	You would understand the principle of law contained in the legislation or case law, and its wider context	You would understand that the river forms a natural barrier, which can be easily identified and defended	You would understand what the symbols in an equation mean and how and when to apply it
Application	You would be able to identify situations to which the principle of law would apply	You might use this knowledge to explain the terms of a peace treaty	You would be able to use the equation to obtain a result, given background information
Analysis	You could relate the facts of a particular scenario to the principle to uncover the extent of its application, using appropriate authority	You could explain the river as a boundary being of importance to the territorial gains/losses for signatories to the peace treaty	You could explain the theoretical process involved in deriving the equation
Synthesis	By a process of reasoning and analogy, you could predict how the law might be applied under given circumstances	You could identify this fact and relate it to the recurrence of this issue in later treaties or factors governing further hostilities and subsequent implications	You would be able to take one equation, link it with another and arrive at a new mathematical relationship or conclusion
Evaluation	You might be able to advise a client based on your own judgement, after weighing up and evaluating all available options	You would be able to discuss whether the use of this boundary was an obstacle to resolving the terms of the treaty to the satisfaction of all parties	You would be able to discuss the limitations of an equation based on its derivation and the underlying assumptions behind this

Can a methodical approach inspire you creatively?

You may doubt this, and we all recognise that a solution to a problem often comes to us when we aren't even trying to think about it. However, technique can sometimes help you clarify the issues, organise the evidence and arrive at a balanced answer. This should help inspiration to follow.

- **Decide exactly the nature of the problem.** An important preliminary task is to make sure you have identified this properly. Write down a description of the problem or issue – if this is not already provided for you – taking care to be very precise with your wording. If a specific statement has been given, then analyse its phrasing carefully to make sure you understand all possible aspects and meanings.

- **Organise your approach to the problem.** You might start with a 'brainstorm' to identify potential solutions or viewpoints. This can be an effective activity. In longer pieces of academic writing such as a dissertation, it might typically consist of three phases:
  - **Open thinking.** Consider the issue or question from all possible angles or positions and write down everything you come up with. Don't worry at this stage about the relevance or importance of your ideas. You may wish to use a 'spider diagram' or 'mind map' to lay out your thoughts (modelled in Figure 10.5).
  - **Organisation.** Next, you should try to arrange your ideas into categories or sub-headings, or group them as supporting or opposing a viewpoint. A new diagram, table or grid may be useful to make things clear.
  - **Analysis.** Now you need to decide about the relevance of the grouped points to the original problem. Reject trivial or irrelevant ideas and rank or prioritise those that seem relevant.

- **Get background information and check your comprehension of the facts.** You will need to gather relevant evidence, information and ideas – to support your thoughts, provide examples or suggest a range of interpretations or approaches. You also need to ensure you fully understand the material you have gathered. This could be as simple as using dictionaries and technical works to find out the precise meaning of key words; it might involve discussing your ideas with your peers or your supervisor; or you could read a range of texts to see how others interpret your topic.

Sharpening your research skills

Consult the following chapters for further information and practical tips:

- Ch 7, for library and web searching
- Ch 17, for plagiarism avoidance strategies
- Ch 18, for collecting information that will allow you to cite sources appropriately

- **Check relevance.** You need to marshal the evidence you have collected - for example: for or against a proposition; supporting or opposing an argument or theory. You may find it useful to prepare a table or grid to organise the information - this will also help you balance your thoughts. Be ruthless in rejecting irrelevant or inconsequential material.

- **Think through your argument, and how you can support it.** Having considered relevant source material and opinions, you should arrive at a personal viewpoint, and then construct your dissertation or project around this. You must take care to avoid value judgements or other kinds of expression of opinion that are not supported by evidence or sources. This is one reason why frequent citation and referencing is demanded in academic work.

What are value judgements?

A value judgement is a statement based primarily on a subjective viewpoint or opinion rather than an objective analysis of facts. It is therefore influenced by the 'value system' of the writer or speaker. Value systems involve such matters as ethics, morals, behavioural norms and religious standpoints that are embedded from someone's upbringing and hence influence their views on external matters, sometimes unwittingly. A value judgement might be detected through the use of 'loaded' language (consider, for example, potentially contrasting usage of 'freedom fighter', 'insurgent' and 'guerrilla'). One aim of academic analysis is to minimise subjectivity of this type by evaluating both sides of a debate and by focussing on the logical interpretation of facts.

● Recognising fallacies and biased presentations

As you consider arguments and discussions on academic subjects, you will notice that various linguistic devices are used to promote particular points of view. Identifying these is a valuable aspect of critical thinking, allowing you to rise above the argument itself and think about the way in which it is being conducted.

Definitions

- **Fallacy:** a fault in logic or thinking that means that an argument is incorrect.
- **Bias:** information that emphasises just one viewpoint or position.
- **Propaganda:** false or incomplete information that supports a (usually) extreme political or moral view.

There are many different types of logical fallacies, and Table 14.3 lists only a few common examples. Once tuned in to this way of thinking, you should observe that faulty logic and debating tricks are frequently used in areas such as advertising and politics. Analysing the methods being used can be a useful way of practising your critical skills.

One way of avoiding bias in your own work is consciously to try to balance your discussion. Avoid 'absolutes' – be careful with words that imply that there are no exceptions, for example, *always*, *never*, *all* and *every*. These words can only be used if you are absolutely sure of facts that imply 100 per cent certainty.

 ## Practical tips for thinking critically

Focus on the task in hand. It is very easy to become distracted when reading around a subject, or when discussing problems with others. Take care not to waste too much time on preliminaries and start relevant action as quickly as possible.

Write down your thoughts. The act of writing your thoughts is important as this forces you to clarify them. Also, since ideas are often fleeting, it makes sense to ensure you have a permanent record. Reviewing what you have written makes you more critical and can lead you on to new ideas.

Table 14.3 **Common examples of logical fallacies, bias and propaganda techniques found in arguments.** There are many different types of fallacious arguments (at least 70) and this is an important area of study in philosophical logic.

Type of fallacy or propaganda	Description	Example	How to counteract this approach
Ad hominem (Latin for 'to the man')	An attack is made on the character of the person putting forward an argument, rather than on the argument itself; this is particularly common in the media and politics	The President's moral behaviour is-suspect, so his financial policies must also be dubious	Suggest that the person's character or circumstances are irrelevant
Ad populum (Latin for 'to the people')	The argument is supported on the basis that it is a popular viewpoint; of course, this does not make it correct in itself	The majority of people support corporal punishment for vandals, so we should introduce boot camps	Watch out for bandwagons and peer-pressure effects and ignore them when considering rights and wrongs
Anecdotal evidence	Use of unrepresentative exceptions to contradict an argument based on statistical evidence	My gran was a heavy smoker and she lived to be 95, so smoking won't harm me	Consider the overall weight of evidence rather than isolated examples
Appeal to authority	An argument is supported on the basis that an expert or authority agrees with the conclusion; used in advertisements, where celebrity endorsement and testimonials are frequent	My professor, whom I admire greatly, believes in Smith's theory, so it must be right	Point out that the experts disagree and explain how and why; focus on the key qualities of the item or argument

Appeal to ignorance	Because there's no evidence for (or against) a case, it means the case must be false (or true)	You haven't an alibi, therefore you must be guilty	Point out that a conclusion either way may not be possible in the absence of evidence
Biased evidence	Selection of examples or evidence for or against a case. A writer who quotes those who support their view, but not those against	My advisers tell me that Global Warming isn't going to happen.	Read around the subject, including those with a different view, and try to arrive at a balanced opinion.
Euphemisms and jargon	Use of phrasing to hide the true position or exaggerate an opponent's - stating things in mild or emotive language for effect; use of technical words to sound authoritative	My job as vertical transportation operative means I am used to being in a responsible position	Watch for (unnecessary) adjectives and adverbs that may affect the way you consider the evidence
Repetition	Saying the same thing over and over again until people believe it. Common in politics, war propaganda and advertising	'A vote for Bloggs is a vote for freedom' 'Your country needs you' 'Beanz means Heinz'	Look out for repeated catchphrases and lack of substantive argument
Straw man/false dichotomy	A position is misrepresented in order to create a diversionary debating point that is easily accepted or rejected, when in fact the core issue has not been addressed	Asylum seekers all want to milk the benefits system, so we should turn them all away	Point out the fallacy and focus on the core issue

171

Try to be analytical, not descriptive. By looking at Table 14.1, you will appreciate why analysis is regarded as a higher-level skill than description. Dissertations can be regarded as weak because the author has simply quoted facts or statements without explaining their importance and context, that is, without showing their understanding of what the quote means or implies.

Ensure that you cite evidence appropriately. This shows you have read relevant source material and helps you avoid plagiarism. The conventions for citation vary among subjects, so consult your regulations and follow the instructions exactly. Make sure that the evidence you quote contributes to the logic of your text.

Draw on the ideas and opinions of your peers and academic staff. Discussions with others can be very fruitful, revealing a range of interpretations that you might not have thought about yourself. You may find it useful to bounce ideas off others. Supervisors can provide useful guidance once you have done some reading, and are usually pleased to be asked for help.

Keep an open mind. Although you may start with preconceived ideas about a topic, you should try to be receptive to the ideas of others. You may find that your initial thoughts become altered by what you are reading and discussing. If there is not enough evidence to support *any* conclusion, be prepared to suspend judgement.

Look beneath the surface. Decide whether sources are dealing with facts or opinions; examine any assumptions made, including your own; think about the motivation of writers. Rather than restating and describing your sources, focus on what they *mean* by what they write.

Avoid common pitfalls of shallow thinking. Try not to:

- rush to conclusions;
- generalise;
- oversimplify;
- personalise;
- use fallacious arguments;
- think in terms of stereotypes; or
- make value judgements.

Keep asking yourself questions. A good way to think more deeply is to ask questions, even after you feel a matter is resolved or you understand it well. All critical thinking is the result of asking questions.

Balance your arguments. To arrive at a position on a subject, consider all possible viewpoints and present your conclusion with supporting evidence.

 And now . . .

14.1 **Practise seeing all sides of an argument.** Choose a topic, perhaps one on which you have strong views (for example, a political matter, such as state support for private schooling; or an ethical one, such as the need for vivisection or abortion). Write down the supporting arguments for different sides of the issue, focussing on your least-favoured option. This will help you see all sides of a debate as a matter of course.

14.2 **Look into the murky world of fallacies and biased arguments.** There are some very good websites that provide lists of different types of these with examples. Investigate these by using 'fallacy' or 'logical fallacies' in a search engine. Not only are the results quite entertaining at times, but you will find the knowledge obtained improves your analytical skills.

14.3 **Look now at a journal article in your subject area.** Read this critically in the sense that you examine it to identify the areas where the authors have relied on the lower-order facets of thinking. Do another 'sweep' over the paper to identify areas where higher-order skills have been used. Consider the balance between those two approaches and reflect on how you will achieve a balance between lower-order and higher-order dimensions in your own dissertation or project report.

Poster presentations

How to display your work effectively

In certain disciplines you may be asked to prepare a poster to summarise research you have done, often as part of a teamwork exercise. The main aim is to develop your communication skills, including how you select and present the content and are able to discuss your work with others.

Key topics:
→ Researching and deciding on content
→ Designing your poster
→ Constructing and setting up a poster
→ Defending your poster

Key terms
Abstract   Peer   Peer assessment   Point size   Poster defence
Rhetorical question

The idea behind a poster display is to present a summary of research or scholarship in an easily assimilated format. Poster sessions are common at academic conferences, particularly in the sciences - they allow many participants to report findings or ideas within a single session and help people with similar interests to meet and discuss detailed information.

The concept has been adapted for undergraduate work for several reasons.

- It allows you to present the results of your work to tutors and fellow students.
- It provides a good end point for teamwork (**Ch 20**).
- It makes you focus on the essence of the topic.
- It develops your presentational skills.
- It allows tutors to observe your verbal communication skills.

Any or all of these aspects may be assessed as part of the exercise. Look into the way marks are divided before you start so that you can allocate your efforts appropriately. If peer assessment is involved, you may wish to discuss this openly at an initial team meeting.

Definition: peer assessment

This is where members of a class assess each other's work. For a poster presentation, members of a group may assess each other's contribution as part of the team, and/or members of the class may judge each other's posters.

The advice presented here will assume that your poster is part of a team exercise where you have been asked to look into a specific aspect of the subject you are studying. The same principles will apply if it is a solo effort, for example if you are reporting the results of a research project.

→ Researching and deciding on content

It might be a good idea for your team first to do a little independent study, so that everyone can gain a general picture of the whole topic. At some point you will want to meet up to decide on the exact focus of your poster, and perhaps allocate specific research tasks for each member. At this stage you should only be thinking about the specific aspects of the topic you feel you need to cover, rather than precise wording. Even seemingly narrow subjects will have scope for different approaches. Although a striking 'take-home message' is important, you should also bear in mind the need for visual impact in your poster when making your choices. There are certain components included in most posters, however, as detailed below.

You will normally be allocated a space to set up your poster (typically 1.5 metre wide and 1 metre high) and, although this may initially seem a large area to cover, you will probably have to select carefully what to include. This is because your poster will need to be legible from a distance of 1 metre or so, and the large font size required for this inevitably means fewer words than you might otherwise prefer. When thinking about content, therefore, it is best to assume that space will be limited.

---

smart tip

Typical components of a poster – a checklist

- ❏ **Title:** phrased in a way that will attract readers' attention
- ❏ **Author information:** names, and in the formal academic type of poster, their affiliation
- ❏ **Abstract or summary:** stating the approach taken and the main conclusions
- ❏ **Introduction:** providing brief background information essential for understanding the poster
- ❏ **Materials and methods:** describing experimental or field research, background theory or historical overview
- ❏ **Results:** key findings or examples
- ❏ **Conclusion:** giving the 'take-home messages' of your study or project
- ❏ **Acknowledgements:** stating who has helped you
- ❏ **References and sources**

→ Designing your poster

The key design principle for your poster is to generate visual impact. It needs to stand out among the others in the session and provide a visual 'hook' to draw a spectator towards the more academic content. This can be achieved in several ways:

Examples of imaginative poster design

- A poster about forest ecology where the text elements are presented as 'leaves' on a model tree.
- A study of urban geography where the poster has the appearance of a street map with aspects written within each building.
- A physiology poster where an organ like the liver is drawn at the centre, with elements attached to it via arteries and veins.

- a striking overall design concept related to the topic;
- effective use of colour or a prominent colour contrast between the background and the poster elements;
- a large image, either attractive or horrific, at the centre of the poster;
- an amusing or punning title;
- some form of visual aid attached to the poster, such as a large model related to the topic.

For convenience, most undergraduate posters are composed of A4 or A3 sheets, or shapes derived from them. These 'panels' will be attached to the main poster board, usually by drawing pins or Velcro pads, and their size or shape may place a constraint on your overall design – check the overall dimensions as soon as you can, to work out your options for arranging these sheets.

The next important aspect to decide is how your readers will work their way through the material you present. Each panel will be read left to right in the usual way, but the route through the panels may not follow this rule. Various options are shown in Figure 60.1. Whichever you choose, it is important to let your readers know which path to take, either by prominent numbering or by incorporating arrows or guidelines into the design.

The ideal text size for your poster title will be about 25-40 mm high (100-170 point size) for the title, 15-25 mm for subtitles (60-100 point) and 5-10 mm (25-40 point) for the main material. If you only have an A4 printer at your disposal, bear in mind that you can enlarge to A3 on most photocopiers, although this may restrict you to black-and-white text. Linear dimensions will increase by 1.41 times if you do this. Once point size and panel dimensions are known, you can work out a rough word limit for each component. When members of the team are working on the content, they will need to bear this limit in mind. Besides being succinct, your writing style should make it easy to assimilate the material, for example, by using bullet points and sub-headings.

smart tip

Group style

We all have our own styles of writing and it is important that you bear this in mind when composing the text, so that idiosyncrasies are ironed out and the overall style is consistent.

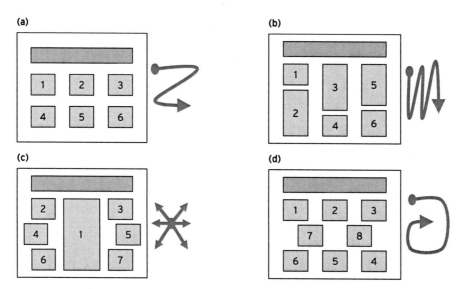

Figure 60.1 **Options for laying out a poster.** The numbers and arrows indicate the route taken by the reader, while the deeper-coloured bar at the top would contain the title and author details.

→ Constructing and setting up a poster

At an early stage, you should draw a diagram of your poster, mapping out the main components to scale. You may also wish to create a mock poster to the exact dimensions to gain a better idea of what the final version will look like.

Each part will need to be printed or copied according to your design brief. Using panels as described above makes it easier to construct the poster as a series of independent components and to bring these to the poster session for final assembly. They can be attached to your board directly or pasted on to card first. You may also wish to laminate each component, or cover it in clear plastic film. A photocopying specialist (see *Yellow Pages* under 'Copying and duplicating services') may be able to carry this out for a charge.

→ Defending your poster

The poster 'defence' for undergraduate work mimics the poster session at a conference where delegates mill around the posters, quizzing the authors about their work. These sessions can be very stimulating for all involved, and collaborations and job offers may result.

If your poster exercise involves an element of defence, it will probably take the form of a 5-10-minute question-and-answer session with your tutors. Expect probing questions to find out how much knowledge and understanding lies behind your presentation, not just what you have selected to display.

Questions about your poster that you should be ready to answer

- Why did you select this topic?
- Who did which part of the research?
- Who thought of the design?
- Who made up the components?
- Can you give me further information on . . . ?
- How does this finding relate to . . . ?
- What does this graph or image mean?
- Where next for this topic or research area?
- How might you improve your poster?

 ## Practical tips for creating better posters

Use the poster title effectively. A two-part title can be used to draw the reader in - the first part being a 'hook' and the second giving more detail. The chapter titles in this book are examples of this approach, but there will be scope for more humour in your poster title, perhaps through a pun on the subject material.

Check out the font sizes you plan to use. Print out a specimen sheet and stand 1-1.5 metres away. You should be able to read the material easily from this distance. Copy some random text (for example, from a website) on to a sheet at the same font size and carry out a word count to gain an idea of what your word limit will be for each component.

Make sure that your poster is able to 'travel well'. You should think about how you take it from the point of construction to the display venue. The components should be portable and packaged in a weather-proof way.

Remember that 'white space' is important in design. An overly fussy presentation with many elements covering the entire area will be difficult to assimilate. In this case, 'less can be more' if it helps you to get your central message across.

Consider colour combinations carefully. Certain colours are difficult to see against others and some pairings may be difficult to distinguish for those who are colour-blind (for example, red and green). Bold, primary colours will attract the eye.

Use imaginative materials. A visit to a craft shop or a do-it-yourself store might give you some ideas. For example, you might see a piece of fabric or single roll of wallpaper at a cheap price that could provide an interesting background.

Use language to draw the reader in. For example, if the titles and sub-headings are given as a series of rhetorical questions, a casual viewer will naturally want to read the text to find out the answer.

Don't provide too much detail. Keep the wording sparse, and be prepared to talk further about matters raised in the text during the poster defence.

Use a handout, if you have too much detail to cover. If you've done lots of research but have to cut some interesting parts out of the final design because of space constraints, consider giving readers a short handout to cover these aspects. This should contain the poster title, author names and contact details.

State your 'take-home message' clearly. Leave your reader in no doubt about your conclusions. You could, for example, list them as a series of bullet points at the end.

Work as a team when answering questions. Be ready to support each other, filling in if someone dries up. However, all members should know the fundamentals of the topic, as any group member may be expected to respond.

GO And now . . .

60.1 Find out the dimensions of your poster space and draw this out to scale. If you copy this sheet your team can use it to sketch out possible designs that will stand a better chance of working.

60.2 Have a critical look at research posters in your department. These are often put up on display after they have been used at a conference. You will probably find them well presented, but some may be rather detailed and formal in appearance. Learn from good and bad aspects of what you see.

60.3 If you are worried about defending your poster, hold a mock event. Prime a flatmate or friend with a series of likely questions (see the checklist on page 435), then try to answer them as you would to your tutors. As well as getting you used to speaking aloud about your work, this should help remove any nervous feelings. It will also allow you to find out what you *don't* know, in time for some quick revision.

Index

183